OXFORD B

Business
Vision

Adrian Wallwork

CONTENTS

UNIT	WORDS AT WORK	GRAMMAR AT WORK	THE INTERVIEW	BUSINESS SKILLS	EMAIL / EXTENDED SPEAKING
7 TRAVEL p66	p66 Travel terms Easily confused words: *travel, trip, journey, bring, take, get, lose, miss*	p69 Past continuous and past perfect **Context:** talking about travel experiences	p70 *easyJet*: European low-cost airline **Listening tip:** sentence stress	p72 Recommending and suggesting travel situations	p74 Email: requests and replies
8 PRODUCTS p76	p80 Marketing 'Buzz' and permission marketing	p78 The passive **Context:** trivia quiz and talking about processes	p76 *Muji*: Japanese retail company **Listening tip:** vowel sounds /iː/ and /ɪ/ sentence stress	p82 Generating and reacting to ideas	p84 Extended speaking: company relocation
9 TRANSACTIONS p86	p88 Understanding headlines, newspaper language	p90 First and second conditionals **Context:** negotiating in everyday life	p86 *Co-operative Bank*: ethical investment **Listening tip:** consonant sounds /v/ /w/ and /h/	p92 Negotiating skills	p94 Email: being clear and brief
10 CUSTOMERS p96	p96 Internet terms talking about websites	p100 *Have to, must,* and *should* **Context:** company culture and office environment	p98 *QXL*: online auction house **Listening tip:** understanding fast speech	p102 Complaining and reassuring	p104 Extended speaking : the merger

Welcome to *Business Vision!*

Business Vision is a course for learners with an approximately intermediate level of English who use, or who are going to use, English in their everyday working lives. It aims to provide the essential vocabulary, grammar structures, and situational language you will need to function in English in a professional environment. The emphasis is on improving communication skills – on the phone, by email, face-to-face over lunch, in meetings, both formal and informal, and standing in front of an audience at a presentation.

The content for *Business Vision* is taken from a wide range of sources: newspapers, journals, reviews, bestselling non-fiction, websites, and original interviews. The author's main priority was to provide interesting, stimulating material and create maximum opportunities for discussion and personalization.

Organization

The Student's Book is divided into ten theme-based units, and there are six sections within each unit. Every unit starts with a *Kick off* section – the function of this is to provide a discussion point to introduce the unit themes. The order and the length of the three middle sections varies from unit to unit. *Words at work* focuses on vocabulary development; *Grammar at work* concentrates on structure; and *The interview* , which is based on an authentic interview with a representative of an innovative modern company, develops aspects of listening skills and pronunciation. The grammar, vocabulary, and speech work they cover feeds into the *Business skills* section which follows them. The final section of each unit is either *Email* (Units 1, 3, 5, and 9) or *Extended speaking activity* (Units 2, 4, 6, 8, and 10).

If the units are studied in sequence, you will gain the maximum benefit from the systematic development of grammar and vocabulary and the recycling and revision built into the syllabus. However, the units also stand alone and could be studied in no particular order according to your own needs and interests.

Kick off

This is the first section of each unit, which is designed to introduce the unit theme. It consists of one or two short discussion questions.

Words at work

All the texts in this section have come from business books, newspapers, or journals. They are authentic, in some cases very slightly adapted, so that you will get a clear idea of what real English is like. The exercises concentrate on word building and collocations work and the aim is to learn and practise core vocabulary related to the unit topic. Glossaries containing explanations of the more difficult words are provided on the page, so that you will not be discouraged by too much unfamiliar vocabulary.

In addition, there is a unit-by-unit *Wordlist* at the back of the book which contains clear, simple definitions of the key vocabulary for each unit topic, (definitions are given the first time a word appears in the book) listed alphabetically with a phonetic transcription. You can learn these core vocabulary lists and use them for revision, whilst teachers can exploit them for vocabulary games, testing, and revision exercises.

Grammar at work

This section teaches and practises core grammar areas within a practical work-related context. Further explanations and additional exercises are in the *Reference section* at the back of the book.

The interview

One of the primary aims of this course is to expose you to real English through live, face-to-face interviews with people from the business world. In most cases, the recordings are originals and what you hear is the interviewee's real voice. When the script has been re-recorded in a studio (in cases where the interview took place over the phone, for example), care has been taken to preserve the words and defining characteristics of the speech of the original interviewee. This section is intended to help you improve your understanding of natural spoken English by identifying and analysing some of its features – for example elision, weak forms, repetition, and redundant utterances – in order to develop strategies for coping with the difficulties they present. There is also work on the vowel and consonant sounds that learners of English typically have the most difficulty in recognizing and producing.

Business skills

This section aims to draw together the grammar and vocabulary in the unit, but concentrates principally on the functional aspects of spoken English – for example what to say on the telephone, how to keep a conversation going with someone you do not know very well, how to participate effectively in a meeting and get people to listen to what you say, etc. It covers tips and techniques for effective communication in these circumstances, as well as the language involved. The *Reference section* contains lists of useful phrases you can use in these contexts.

Email

The email writing sections at the end of Units 1, 3, 5, 7, and 9 take you through a complete email-writing course, which covers the basic techniques and language needed to write clear and effective emails in the most appropriate style. The *Reference section* contains a list of standard phrases which you can use in emails.

Extended speaking

The extended speaking activities at the ends of Units 2, 4, 6, 8 and 10 give you the opportunity to practise your newly acquired skills and language in a variety of meeting scenarios.

Other features of the course

Factoids

The factoids are the interesting facts and statistics quoted in the margin on many pages of the Student's Book. They relate to the general theme of the unit and their purpose is to give further examples of or information about the subject being covered, and to promote discussion. The Teacher's Book contains ideas for further exploitation of the factoids.

Audio material and tapescripts

The listening material for the Student's Book is available on both audio cassette and CD. The tapescripts are at the back of the Student's Book, beginning on page 138.

Teacher's Book

In addition to a step-by-step guide to using the Student's Book material in the classroom, the 96-page Teacher's Book contains answers to all the exercises, tips for teaching difficult language points and a wealth of ideas for lead-in and extension activities. It also provides four progress tests with answers and ten pages of extra photocopiable activities.

Workbook

The activities in the Workbook – which include exercises, quizzes, reading comprehension exercises, wordsearches, and crosswords – consolidate, practise, and extend the areas of language taught in the Student's Book.

Website (www.oup.com/elt/businessvision)

The website provides further practice and extension of the themes and language taught in the Student's Book in the form of interactive exercises, games, and activities. Other add-ons include an interactive glossary.

Modern business life
The Photographers Library/photolibrary.com

1 IMAGES OF BUSINESS

KICK OFF

1 Look at the picture above. What do you think it is trying to say about the modern world of business?

2 What do you think makes a modern company successful? Put the following in order of importance. Then compare with a partner.

a high-quality products and services

b good people management

c aggressive marketing and advertising

d fast reaction to change

WORDS AT WORK

Doing business

The texts below are from a book by two Swedish business experts about helping your businesses to succeed in the new global economy.

3 Read the texts and match with the headings *a–d* below.

a New management

b Brain power

c Be different!

d Do it faster, do it now!

1
intellect (*n*) – ability to think, intelligence
critical (*adj*) – most important

2
wild (*adj*) – not in control
differentiate yourself (*v*) – to be different
increasingly difficult (*adj*) – more and more difficult
unique (*adj*) – the only one like this
innovate (*v*) – to introduce new ideas / ways of doing things

1

Workers now control the principal means of production. In a modern company 70 to 80 per cent of what people do, is done using their intellects. The critical means of production is small, grey, and weighs around 1.3 kilograms. It is the human brain.

2

In the wild market economy which now exists it is increasingly difficult to differentiate yourself. If you think about it, most of what your business does could be bought from someone else using the Yellow Pages or an Internet search engine. If you have a unique idea your competitors will steal it in two or three weeks … There is only one way out. Do something that the world has not seen before. Innovate, so that what you are, for a moment in time, is unique and uniquely competitive.

3

renewal (n) – making new improvement
apply to (v) – to concern or relate to
launch (v) – to introduce a new product

4

critical (adj) – important
key (n) – the thing that makes something possible

3

The need for renewal is something that applies to everything in an organization; it concerns everyone, goes on everywhere and is non-stop. ...

Move it:
In 1995, 1,000 new soft drinks were launched on the Japanese market. A year later, 1 per cent of them were still for sale.

Move it faster:
At Hewlett Packard, the majority of revenues come from products that did not exist a year ago.

Move it now:
In Tokyo, you can order a customized Toyota on Monday and be driving it on Friday.

4

The most critical resource a business has wears shoes and walks out of the door around five o'clock every day. As a result, management and leadership are keys to competitive advantage. How you attract, train, and motivate your people is more important than technology. ...The boss is dead. No longer can we believe in a leader who claims to know more about everything and who is always right.

2 Read the texts again. Are the following true (T) or false (F)?

1 What most people do at work all day is use their brains.
2 Because of the Internet, it is now easier to be different and unique.
3 Hewlett Packard makes most money from products launched last year.
4 A company will be more competitive if it manages its employees well.
5 A strong boss is important in good management.

3 Read the texts once more, and use them to help you complete the table below, as in the example. All the words you need are in the texts.

verb	adjective	noun	noun (person)
to produce	productive	product / _____ 4	producer
to compete	_____ 3	competition	_____ 7
differentiate 1	different	difference	
to lead	leading	_____ 5	_____ 8
_____ 2	innovative	innovation	innovator
to manage	managing	_____ 6	manager

4 Underline the correct word in the sentences below. Then ask and answer the questions with a partner.

1 Who is the market *leader / leadership* and the main *innovation / innovator* in your field of business?
2 How much *competitive / competition* is there?
3 What are your company's main *products / produce* and services? How do you *difference / differentiate* them from your *competitors / competition*?
4 Can you describe your company's *managing / management* structure? Draw a diagram to help you.
5 Who are your main *customs / customers* and *suppliers / supplies*?

Products are becoming more and more similar. The final report for 1996 of the rating institute, JD Power began with the observation that 'There are no bad cars any longer, because they are all good.'
Funky Business

GRAMMAR AT WORK

Present simple vs present continuous

1 What is your 'dream' job?

1 Divide the list of jobs below into 'nightmare' or 'dream' jobs. Give reasons for your choice. Can you think of anything positive about the nightmare jobs, and negative about the dream ones?

deep-sea diver	film director	promotions manager for a pop group
accountant	wine grower	aid worker in a war zone
archeologist	taxi driver	secondary school teacher

2 Can you think of any others for each list?

(((1.1))) **2** You are going to hear the two people below describing their jobs. Make sure you understand the words in the list, then listen and complete the first two columns in the table below.

core business (*n*) – the most important activity of a company
turn up (*v*) (informal) – to arrive, or appear, e.g. at a meeting
scheduling (*n*) from to schedule (*v*) – to plan when things will happen, timetable
to promote – to publicize and sell (a product or service)
tedious (*adj*) – boring
tax avoidance (*n*) – finding ways not to pay your taxes

	interviewee 1	interviewee 2	you
job title			
where company is			
type of company			
number of employees			
responsible for …			
usually does …			
currently doing …			

3 Listen again and write down the positive and negative aspects of each job. Then fill in the third column in the table with information about yourself.

4 Read the sets of questions and answers below.

1 *Do you live* in New York?

2 It's 10 p.m. Why *are you working* now?

3 So *are you living* in New York?

4 Who *do you work* for?

a *A record company in New York.*

b *Yes. I've lived here all my life.*

c *I've got a presentation tomorrow.*

d *Yes, for the moment, but I'll probably go back to Rome next year.*

1 Match questions 1–4 with answers *a–d*.

2 Which questions are in the present simple and which are in the present continuous?

3 Complete the rules in the box below.

The present _____ is used to talk about permanent situations and regular actions.

The present _____ to talk about temporary situations (which are on-going), and actions that are happening now, this moment.

▶ **For more on the present tenses, see the Reference section pages 129–30.**

5 Look at the list of work situations below. Decide which tense – present simple (PS) or present continous (PC) – you would use for each situation.

Then write example sentences based on your own job and company.

1 presenting factual information about the company. PS

e.g. We specialize in the production of chemicals used in the paper industry.

2 describing the current progress in a project

3 explaining why someone can't come to the phone

4 explaining how a product works

5 explaining the frequency of an event, routine, or habit

6 Write questions about your partner's job and company using the present simple or continuous of the verbs in brackets. Then take it in turns to ask and answer the questions.

1 Where your company (*have*) office? They (*plan*) to open any new office?

2 How big (*be*) the company? How many people (*employ*) it?

3 What (*be*) the core business? Which products services currently (*sell*) best?

4 What (*be*) the role your division department in the company?

5 You (*like*) your job? What you (*be*) responsible for? Who you (*be*) responsible to?

6 What kind of problems you (*have to*) resolve? What sort of problems you (*deal*) with at the moment?

7 Which of your talents and skills you currently not (*use*) much? Why?

8 What project you (*work*) on now? How it (*go*)?

7 Prepare a brief presentation to the class about your job and your company using the information in the table in **2**. Try to think of two or three things to say for each heading. Remember to speak slowly and clearly.

A survey found that 70% of staff believed the people they met outside work instantly judged them by their job title, and that many would be willing to forgo an increase in salary for a more 'professional sounding' position.

The Times

THE INTERVIEW

St Luke's advertising agency

Name: Juliet Soskice
Position: Marketing Manager
Company: St Luke's
Field of Business: Advertising

1 You are going to hear about St Luke's, a highly successful advertising agency in London with an unusual working environment. What is your ideal working environment? Do the quiz below – you can choose one or more answers for each category.

2 Compare answers with a partner. How much is your current working environment like your ideal. How is it different?

YOUR IDEAL WORKING ENVIRONMENT

1 Type of company: **a** state-owned **b** publicly traded **c** small **d** medium **e** multinational **f** start-up

2 Type of job: **a** routine, but secure **b** challenging, but not secure **c** people-oriented **d** creative

3 Management style: **a** traditional and formal **b** informal 'flat' management hierarchy

4 Working hours: **a** flexible **b** fixed **c** part time **d** work from home **e** long **f** short

5 Salary related to: **a** experience / length of service **b** hours actually worked **c** performance **d** commission

6 The way employees' concerns are voiced is by: **a** trade union **b** elected committees of employees **c** directly to superiors **d** anonymously **e** other (which?)

7 Offices: **a** open-plan **b** cubicles **c** own office **d** hot-desking (no allocated desks)

8 Office facilities: **a** coffee machine **b** a smoking room **c** lockers **d** showers **e** canteen

9 Free flow of information regarding: **a** all company business **b** only some company business **c** everything apart from salaries and personal data

10 Perks and benefits: **a** company car **b** subsidized canteen food **c** stock options **d** private medical insurance/healthcare **e** gym or club membership **f** other (which?)

Listen to Juliet talking about her unusual working environment. Tick (✓) the factors she mentions from the quiz in the boxes provided.

4 Listen again and answer the questions.

1 How many employees are there in the elected committee?
2 Where does Juliet keep her personal things?
3 Which employees have their own offices?
4 What do employees do first when they arrive at work in the morning?
5 What did Ericsson design specially for St Lukes?
6 Who do the 'brand rooms' belong to? What are they for?
7 Which of these clients are mentioned: HFPC, HSBC, APC, IPC, IDEA, IKEA?
8 Is it possible to find out what a colleague's salary is?
9 What other perks – apart from the gym, healthcare, and the canteen – does Juliet mention?

5 Listening tip

Because we think faster than we can express ourselves, we often speak in incomplete sentences and repeat things. In the extracts below underline all the examples you can find of:

– repetition   – incomplete sentences
– hesitation noises (*er, um*)   – unnecessary extra phrases (*you know, I mean*)

Q: And what about the office environment, how important is that? Because obviously looking round me here it is quite a different, different place to work.
A: Well, um, the most important element in this office is, is, in the sense that there is no office.
Q: And what about perks? Are there any company perks that … ?
A: I think the greatest perk is, I mean, let me tell you what the perks are, yes, very good healthcare.

(((1.3))) **6** Now listen to another extract taken from later on in the interview where Juliet is talking about her working hours.

1 The first time you listen, notice the amount of hesitation, repetition, and redundant language.
2 Listen a second time and try to focus on the main message. Write a two-sentence summary of the main points that she makes. Compare your result with a partner.
3 Now check your answer with the tapescript on page 139. Notice that you only need to understand a small percentage of the language in order to grasp the main message.

7 Talking point

Juliet talks about the need to have mobile phones at St Luke's. How important is a mobile phone for you – both for work and personal use?

When talking to other native speakers, the average person only listens at about 25% of his or her potential. This means that we ignore, distort, or forget 75% of what we hear. Surprisingly this doesn't seem to interfere with our understanding.

A Guide to Listening

EMAIL

Beginnings and endings

1 Are the statements below true (T) or false (F)? Answer for yourself, then compare your answers with a partner.

1 I have had email for more than five years.
2 Electronic writing is completely different from traditional writing.
3 Email has changed the way I work and communicate with friends.
4 I rarely use the phone and write letters now that I have email.
5 Formal emails are more difficult to write than informal emails.
6 It is acceptable to use email at work for private uses.
7 Employers have the right to monitor emails sent by their employees.

2 The table below shows possible ways to begin and end an email.

1 Which expressions could you use in a business email to McKenzie James, a potential customer whom you have never met before?
2 Are there any expressions which you would probably not use in a letter?

Salutation	Name	Introduction
Hi	Mr McKenzie	The reason I'm writing is …
Good morning	Ms James	Your name was given to me by …
Dear	McKenzie James	I am writing to you to …
Hello	McKenzie	I am the Sales Manager at …
nothing	nothing	This is just to let you know that …

Conclusion	Final salutation
I look forward to hearing from you.	Best / Kind regards
Hear from you soon.	Best
If you need any further information, do not hesitate to contact us.	Cheers
nothing	Yours sincerely
	All the best
	nothing

3 Look at the extracts from emails below.

1 Decide whether you think each is a beginning or an ending, and if the style is formal or neutral, as in the examples.
  a Re your inquiry. *beginning, neutral*
  b Please accept my sincere apologies for having to cancel our meeting. *beginning, formal*
  c Good luck with the presentation.
  d Thanks for yr message.
  e Following our telephone conversation of today, I enclose our offer to provide you with …
  f Kindly give the matter your prompt attention.
  g Thank you in advance for any help you may be able to give me.
  h I am looking forward to seeing you.
  i I write to inform you that …
  j Say hello to Pete.

According to the Society for Human Resource Management, more than 36% of employers look at employees' email and over 70% believe it is an employer's right to read anything in the company's electronic communication system.
Personnel Today

2 Rewrite each extract in either a more formal or a more informal way, as in the examples.

a *With regard to your inquiry.* (formal version)

b *I'm really sorry I had to cancel our meeting.* (informal version)

4 Discuss the questions below with a partner before checking the answers in the cyber tip.

1 How could you begin first contact emails to the following business people: Ludmila Davidovna Garanina from Moscow, Yuji Amamoto from Tokyo, Lee Kun Hee from Seoul. Compare with the key on page 106.

2 What could you do if you don't know the exact name of the person you want to email, or if you are sending information to an entire team or department?

3 Most first emails are quite formal. How do you decide when you can become less formal?

I'm just phoning to check that you received my email!

YOU'VE GOT MAIL!

CYBERTIP

Beginning an email correspondence

✦ At the start of your message say:
  1 How you found their name (if they don't know you).
  2 Who you are (position and company).
  3 What you want.
  4 Why your correspondent should be interested.

✦ Remember that the order first name, surname is not standard throughout the world.

✦ If in doubt, use person's full name and avoid *Mr / Mrs / Ms*, e.g. *Dear Andrea Ferrari*.

✦ When writing to an entire department or team you can use *Dear All* or *For the attention of the Marketing Team*.

✦ When sending a first email only use an informal style with people you already know. When replying, match the formality and style of the sender.

✦ Use an automatic signature – which gives your name, title / position / company at the end of each email.

---

5 Write an email to Hiro Wada in Osaka who has written to your company asking for information about your products and services.

6 Exchange emails with a partner. Try to improve and correct each other's work.

7 Now rewrite your email in an informal style. A friend you met in a chatroom, Maria Adzima, has asked you to describe your company and job.

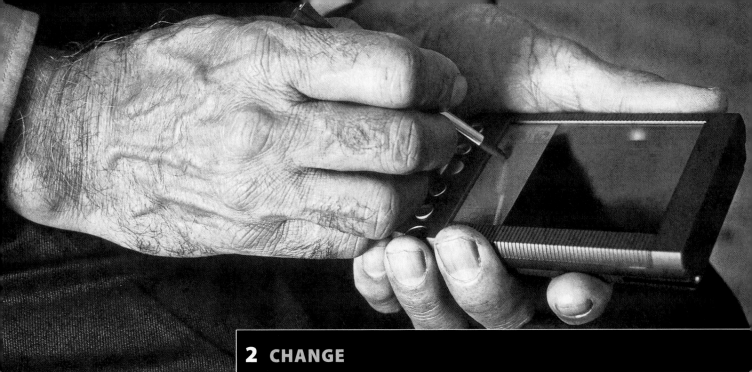

2 CHANGE

KICK OFF

1 Look at the picture. What does it tell you about the way technology is changing working life?

2 How much time, on average, do you spend on the Internet a day at work and at home? Compare with a partner.

WORDS AT WORK

E-commerce

3 Read quickly through the text about Amazon. Underline three things about Amazon or Jeff Bezos that you didn't know before or that interest you. Compare with a partner.

4 Read the text again and find the following information.

1 The rate at which Internet use was growing when Bezos decided to set up Amazon.
2 How probable Bezos thought it was that Amazon would succeed.
3 The number of books in the first Amazon catalogue.
4 Two reasons why 'one-click shopping' was successful.
5 The location of the warehouse which serviced Amazon customers in Asia.
6 Two things, apart from the actual books, that the early customers of Amazon could find on the website.
7 The two areas Bezos invested heavily in.
8 The reason why it was particularly essential Amazon to grow fast and be on a large scale.
9 Two languages, other than English, in which Amazon customers can buy books.
10 Two products, other than books, that Amazon now sells.

Amazon
– Pioneers in e-commerce

pioneer (n) – a person who is the first to develop something
retirement (n) – period of your life after you stop working
set up (v) – to begin or establish a business
set out to – to begin to do something with a particular aim / goal
obsession (n) – one particular idea or thing that you think about all the time
mantra (n) – a word / sound which you repeat again and again, like a prayer
to go bust (adj) – when a business loses all its money

The founder and CEO of Amazon is a former Wall Street banker, Jeff Bezos. In the early 90s, he noticed that use of the Internet was growing by over 2000% per month. So, he borrowed his parents' retirement savings (around $300 000, which he told them they had a 70% chance of losing) and set up a company to sell books online.

1.1 MILLION BOOKS
Bezos opened the virtual doors of Amazon.com's online bookstore in July 1995 with a catalogue of no less than 1.1 million books. 'We set out to offer customers something they simply could not get in any other way,' he says. 'We brought much more selection than was possible in a physical store (our store would now occupy six football fields) and presented it in a useful easy-to-search format in a store open 365 days a year, 24 hours a day.'

SELLING TO THE WORLD WITH ONE-CLICK SHOPPING
Amazon enjoyed great success almost from the start. The company had only two distribution centres but they shipped books across the whole world – the centre in Seattle serviced the West Coast of the United States and

Asia, the one in Delaware serviced the East Coast and Europe. The user-friendliness and efficiency of Amazon's pioneering 'one-click shopping' technology meant that customers who tried buying books online for the first time often came back for more.

AN OBSESSION WITH CUSTOMERS
'Obsess about customers, not competitors' was Bezos's motto in the early days. 'Most of the customers out there haven't bought anything online', he said in an interview in 1998. 'We want to be their first purchase if we can. We want to have a very deep relationship with them.' Bezos made the Amazon website more than just a place to buy books. He created a community of and for book lovers – with book reviews from readers, news about the latest publications, even the first interactive novel. (American novelist John Updike wrote the first chapters, and site visitors completed the story.)

GET BIG FAST
Apart from customers, Bezos's other obsession was growth. 'Our major strategic objective has always been GBF', he declared. 'It's a mantra inside

the company and it means Get Big Fast.' Amazon invested heavily in advertising to attract new customers and in developing online software. The company grew, but made greater losses every quarter. This didn't seem to worry Bezos. His idea was that the return for the huge 'fixed cost' investment in software would eventually come from Amazon's continuously growing customer base.

STILL EXCITED
Many of the early dotcoms went bust, and the business world began to lose confidence in e-commerce. Amazon however, expanded into Europe and diversified into music and toys. By the last quarter of 2000 it did finally begin to make a profit. Bezos remains optimistic: 'We have made it possible for anyone in the world to buy a German language book or a Japanese language book', he says proudly. He is still excited by the possibilities of selling on the Net 'Because it's a scale business where costs are largely fixed, if we can have the largest scale, we can have the best prices and the best service', he explains, 'which in the physical world would be impossible.'

⑤ Cover the text and try to complete the sentences below with the correct form of the verbs in the box, as in the example.

expand	invest	lose	borrow	diversify	ship
distribute	grow				

1 Bezos _borrowed_ money from his parents to set up Amazon.
2 The new company was very successful and _____ very rapidly, but _____ money.
3 Amazon _____ books to the whole world from two _____ centres in the United States.
4 Bezos has _____ lots of money in advertising and online software development.
5 Amazon has _____ into other products as well as books, including toys and music.
6 The company has _____ into Europe and Japan.

⑥ Which of the following Internet services **a** do you use, and **b** does your company use? Compare with a partner and discuss the advantages and disadvantages of each.

1 booking airline tickets / theatre tickets
2 job finding / recruiting personnel
3 food shopping
4 shopping for other items (what?)
5 news and information services
6 chat rooms

A six country survey revealed that the average age of online buyers is 38, over 50% are married, the majority are male, and most are graduates. The top three items bought are computers, books, and CDs, and the favourite site shopped (i.e. not just visited) in all six countries is Amazon.
Ernst and Young

GRAMMAR AT WORK

Present perfect vs present simple

1 Look at the sentences 1–4 and explanations *a–d* below.

1 *This is the first time I***'ve used** *this program.*
2 *The first time I* **use** *a new program it never works.*
3 *How long* **have you been** *here?*
4 *How long* **are** *you here for?*

a I want to know when you will leave.
b I want to know when you arrived.
c This software is new to me.
d I generally have problems with software.

1 Match each sentence with the appropriate explanation.
2 Which sentences are in the present simple tense, and which are in the present perfect tense?
3 Complete the rule in the box below.

The _____ _____ is used to connect a present situation to a past event.
The _____ _____ is used to talk about the present, including situations that occur again and again.

▶ **For more on the present perfect, see the Reference section page 127.**

2 Read the sentences below, and note the difference between *for* and *since*.

I've been with the company **for six years**. (focus on length of time)
I've been a project manager **since last year**. (focus on when the situation began)

1 Now complete the sentences below with *for* or *since*.
  a He's only been in the job _____ May 2002.
  b I haven't seen him _____ a long time.
  c I haven't had a holiday _____ I started work.
  d I worked abroad _____ several years.
  e The new office has been open _____ 10 March.
  f She hasn't enjoyed her job as much _____ she had a baby.

2 Ask your partner how long he / she has had his / her:
  a house / flat   **b** car   **c** current job   **d** email

Present perfect vs past simple

3 Look at these two sentences. Which is in the present perfect and which is in the past simple?

1 *Jeff Bezos* **founded** *Amazon in 1995.*
2 *The company* **has expanded** *into Europe and diversified.*

Complete the rule in the box below.

The _____ is used to talk about finished actions in finished periods of time.
The ——— is used to talk about ongoing or unfinished situations in ongoing or unfinished periods of time.

One in three British men and one in ten women now work 50 or more hours a week. Two-thirds of UK managers believe that long hours are harming their health, relationships, and productivity. Stress is the biggest problem for European companies and in Japan work-related suicides have doubled since 1970.
Personnel Today

④ Look at the questions and answers below.

1 **Have you** ever **bought** anything online?
2 When **did you** first **buy** a computer?
3 **Have you used** the Web today?
4 **Did you use** the Web yesterday?

a *No, the network was down all day.*
b *Just a few books and CDs.*
c *In 1991, a Macintosh.*
d *So far, only to download some software.*

1 Match questions 1–4 with answers a–d.
2 Which tense is used for specific moments in the past?

⑤ Match each work situation 1–6 with an example sentence a–e. Which tense is used – present perfect (PP), or past simple (PS)? See the example.

1 presenting the major events in the history of a company *b* PS
2 explaining the impact of a piece of new technology on company business
3 talking about the duration until now of a specific situation
4 talking about your career / life experiences without specifying exact dates
5 giving the results of last year's business
6 describing the progress so far in a project

a *I've been with the company for six years, and since last year I've been a project manager.*

b *The company was founded in 2001 by a group of software engineers.*

c *In the first quarter revenues increased by nearly 50 per cent.*

d *Well, we've covered the first three milestones, and we're still on schedule.*

e *I think the Internet has completely revolutionized the way we interface with customers.*

f *I've worked on several biotechnology projects, and have been involved in systems development.*

⑥ Write questions about your partner's company. Use the correct tense (present or past simple, present perfect) of the verbs in italics. Then ask and answer the questions with your partner.

1 When (*be*) your company founded?
2 Who (*be*) the CEO? How long he / she (*be*) CEO? Who (*be*) CEO before?
3 Company (*expand / diversify*) since it (*be*) founded?
4 How much impact (*have*) Internet on how your company works?
5 What (*be*) your main role in your company? How long you (*have*) that role? What you (*do*) before?
6 What other work experience you (*have*)? You for any other companies? (*work*)
7 Your company's revenues (*increase*) last year? What product / service (*be*) your biggest seller?
8 How many projects you (*be*) involved in since joined company? What progress (*make*) in your current project?

⑦ Prepare and present a short summary of either: **a** the history and milestones of your company, or **b** your work experience.

THE INTERVIEW

Ferrari

Name: Tim Watson
Position: International Press and PR Manager
Company: Ferrari
Field of Business: Sports cars
Head Office: Maranello, Italy

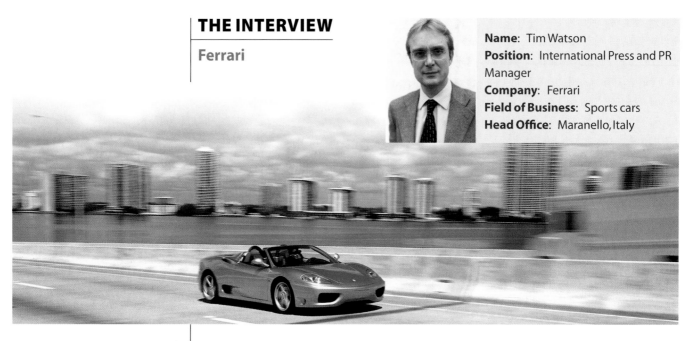

❶ How much do you know about Ferrari? Read the text and find:

1 how many cars the company produces a year.
2 how long it takes to assemble a car.
3 how Ferraris can be customized.
4 how long you have to wait for a Ferrari driving course.
5 the different types of Ferrari customer.

FERRARI
FACTS AND FIGURES

1 Ferrari operate in 43 countries. The US is the largest market, followed by Germany and the UK. Total annual sales output is limited to about 3,500 cars.

2 All Ferraris are hand-made. None of the production process is automated. When each separate part of the car is finished, it takes about three days to assemble the car itself.

3 Customers can have their Ferraris customized. Features that can be customized include the seats, the dashboard, and colour of the stitching on the upholstery (made from the hide of three cows).

4 Ferrari mechanics use a wind tunnel to improve performance. If they succeed in increasing the speed by even half a second, they are considered to have done a good job.

5 Many features of the road cars derive from technologies developed for Formula 1 driving. In fact the road cars can be driven on the road or on the racing circuit.

6 There is a two-year waiting list for three-day intensive Ferrari driving courses.

7 Ferrari has three very different customer types: wealthy clients who buy the cars plus expensive merchandising (steering wheel replicas, gold watches, etc.), racing fans who buy hats and T shirts, and children. 35% to 40% of the merchandise is aimed at this age group.

(((2.1))) **❷** Now you are going to hear about the early history of Ferrari. Listen to Tim Watson and answer the questions below.

1 When was the first Ferrari made?
2 When was the company created?
3 When did Enzo Ferrari build his own first car?
4 Who did he build it under licence to?
5 Does the first car still exist?
6 Why did Ferrari sell his cars after racing them?
7 Why was the first Ferrari red?
8 When did Ferrari start making cars in other colours?

(((2.2))) ③ You are going to hear Tim talking about his job as International Press and PR Manager for Ferrari. Listen the first time and write down two things he does or is responsible for in his new job, and one thing he finds particularly interesting.

④ Listen again and answer the questions.

1 How many people work at Ferrari?
2 What happened at Silverstone recently, and what was Tim responsible for in this situation?
3 What two things do the journalists who come to the factory want to do?
4 Why do things change quickly at Ferrari?
5 How long has Tim worked for Ferrari in Italy and what was his job in England?

Listening tip

(((2.3))) ⑤ The -ed ending of the simple past and past participle can be pronounced in three different ways. Listen to the pronunciation of *offered*, *worked*, and *created* then practise saying the three sounds aloud.

/d/ offered	/t/ worked	/ɪd/ created

(((2.4))) ⑥ Put the verbs below into the correct column of the table. Then listen and check your answers.

watched	joined	happened	experienced
remembered	stressed	restricted	followed
launched	studied	moved	developed

⑦ Say the verbs aloud, and write down the number of syllables. Then listen again and check your answers.

e.g. *looked* – /lʊkt/ = one syllable. The 'e' is silent.

(((2.5))) ⑧ Listen to these words – what happens to the vowels in bold?

1 b**u**siness   2 second**a**ry   3 diff**e**rent

(((2.6))) ⑨ Cross out the vowels in the words below that are not usually pronounced. Then listen and check your answers. Practise reading the words aloud.

1 secretary   3 Wednesday   5 comfortable   7 personal
2 interesting   4 preferable   6 temperature   8 average

Talking point

⑩ Tim Watson talks about the speed of change at Ferrari. How quickly do / can things change in your company? What has changed since you joined the company? What changes would you like to see?

clean
delicious
free
fresh
full
good
new
special
sure
wonderful

① To the left is a list of the ten most frequently used adjectives in advertising.

1 Write the comparative and superlative form of each adjective.
2 The list of adjectives is not in order. Decide what you think the five most frequently used adjectives are. Compare with the key on page 106.
3 Which could be used to describe the product or service that your company offers? What other adjectives would be more appropriate?

②

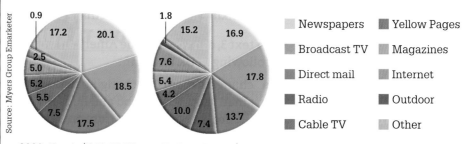

Source: Myers Group Emarketer

■ Newspapers	■ Yellow Pages
■ Broadcast TV	■ Magazines
■ Direct mail	■ Internet
■ Radio	■ Outdoor
■ Cable TV	■ Other

2000 Total: $242.9 billion   **Today** Total: $277.4 billion

Use the information above (about spending on different types of advertising) to help you complete the sentences with expressions from the box.

| a little less | quite a lot more | as | than | as | three times as much |
| far more | the same amount | than | than | as | twice as much |

1 Today advertisers spend about _____ on Internet advertising _____ they did in 2000.
2 There is about _____ spent on magazine advertising now _____ there was in 2000.
3 There is _____ spent on cable TV advertising _____ there was in 2000.
4 Advertisers now spend _____ on radio advertising _____ they did in 2000.
5 Today there is exactly _____ spent on outdoor advertising _____ there was in 2000.
6 In 2000 there was _____ spent on direct mail advertising _____ there is today.

Describing trends

3 Read about some current trends. Choose what you think is the correct answer from the verbs in italics. Compare with the key on page 106.

1 In most European countries, unemployment has been steadily *increasing / decreasing* since 1993, but so too has the number of people employed in industries such as agriculture, coal mining, shipbuilding, and steel.

2 The amount of paper consumed in offices is going *down / up* quite rapidly.

3 The population of some industrial countries (e.g. Japan and Italy) is *falling / rising*. They will need between 5,000–6,500 immigrants a year to maintain the current worker / pensioner ratio.

4 The number of women in the workforce has *dropped / grown* by 24.2% since 1992.

5 In many countries income tax has *decreased / increased* by between 10 and 20 times since 1900.

4 In the box are some of the verbs that are used to describe trends. Put them into the correct column in the table, as in the examples.

| go up | decrease | go down | fall | worsen | fluctuate |
| peak | recover | drop | increase | rise | improve |

↘	↗	⌄⌄
go down		
		⌃

5 We use adjectives and adverbs to describe the type and speed of change.
*e.g. There has been a **steady** decrease in unemployment.*
*The amount of paper consumed in offices is going up quite **steadily**.*

Complete the table and fill in the gaps in the description of the graph with the correct adjectives and adverbs.

adjective	adverb
steady	steadily
slight	
sharp	
considerable	
dramatic	

Sales started high in January, and rose _____ [1] throughout the first quarter of the year. Then there was a _____ [2] drop in April when our Los Angeles distributors went out of business. Sales rose _____ [3] throughout May and June, as the US market began to recover, but fell again _____ [4] in July when there was a fire in our warehouse in Mexico City. From this low point, sales rose fairly steadily until the end of the year, with a _____ [5] increase in December corresponding with the Christmas promotion period.

$ millions | US and Latin American sales figures for last year

5'
4.5'
4'
3.5'
3'
2.5'
2'
1.5'
1'
0.5

J F M A M J J A S O N D

BUSINESS SKILLS

Presentations

1 Have you ever seen a particularly good or bad presentation, or given one yourself? Compare with a partner. Then make a list of five tips to give someone who is going to give their first presentation.

2 Now try this quiz and check your answers with the key on page 106.

The 5th Wave   By Rich Tennant

Could you be an expert presenter?

1 What is the ideal length of a presentation?
  a 30 minutes
  b 50 minutes
  c 90 minutes
  d 120 minutes

2 How much time should you spend on preparation? For each minute of presentation:
  a 5 minutes of preparation
  b 20 minutes
  c 30 minutes
  d 60 minutes

3 Which of the following do you need to know about your audience? (Choose one or more.)
  a why they are there
  b their age
  c their business background
  d their cultural background

4 Which element of a presentation has the greatest impact on the audience?
  a the way they see you as a presenter
  b your visual aids
  c your voice
  d the content itself

5 Do people retain information best if they:
  a hear it?
  b read it?
  c see it?

6 At which point/s in a presentation do people remember most effectively?
  a the beginning
  b the middle
  c the end
  d the beginning and end

7 How many points should you make?
  a as many as you can
  b between 5 and 10
  c only those key points that are absolutely essential

8 In a short presentation is it best to
  a present a broad-based area?
  b focus on a narrow specific subject?

9 How many visual aids should you use?
  a one every minute
  b one every 2 minutes
  c 5 minutes
  d 10 minutes

10 Which is the most important for an effective presentation?
  a rehearsal
  b a positive approach
  c not feeling nervous
  d audience management

(((3.4))) **3** Listen to Martin Addison of Video Arts giving some brief presentation tips.

1 What does he say is the first step in preparing a presentation?
2 What advice does he give about the general approach to adopt?
3 What does he say about beginnings and endings?

(((3.5))) **4** Look at the presentation structure on the opposite page. Listen to some extracts from a presentation and match the extracts *a–f* with the stages 1–6.

a   2   b ___   c ___   d ___   e ___   f ___

PRESENTATION STRUCTURE

1 Introduce yourself.
2 Give the topic and length of presentation.
3 Explain how the presentation is organized.
    i First topic X.
    ii Then topic Y.
    iii Finally topic Z.
    iv Tell audience when to ask questions.
4 Do it.
    i Talk about topic X.
    ii Summarize topic X.
    iii Introduce topic Y.
    iv Talk about topic Y, etc.
5 Summarize the main points of the whole presentation.
6 Conclude and questions.

(((3.6))) **5** Now listen to the whole talk and check your answers. Then listen again and try to fill in the gaps in the expressions below:

1 Begin:

I'd like_____
myself. I'm Tim Jackson and I'm ...

2 Introduce topic:

I'm _____ about
how we can boost your sales figures.

3 Explain organization of talk:

In _____, I will
focus on the trends in TV advertising
over ... . Finally, _____
our recommendations. If you
_____ , please save them
for the end.

4 Refer to visual aids:

As_____ slide, the
least persuasive types of ads last
year ...

AND IN THE THIRD PART OF MY PRESENTATION

5 Move on to a new topic:

... endorse products.
This_____ most important
part, our recommendations.

6 Recap (summarize):

So_____
points I would like you to remember
from my talk today ...

7 Wrap up (conclude):

Well that _____ talk.
_____for listening.
Now _____
questions?

Compare with a partner before checking with the tapescript on page 142.

6 Choose one of the topics below and prepare a short presentation based on the points provided.

1 a progress report of a project you are working on – project description, progress to date, outstanding work, action plan.
2 a feature of your company you would like to change – background to company, why this change? effects of change, action plan.
3 your ambitions for the future – your position now, where you want to be, how you're going to achieve it, how long it will take you.

EMAIL

Levels of formality

1 Look at the following different kinds business correspondence. Which would you not send by email? Why?

a a price estimate
b a job application
c a formal complaint
d confirmation of a contract
e request to arrange a meeting
f an enquiry about a product

2 Formal written English is more indirect than spoken English (e.g. *I was wondering if you could* ... instead of simply *could you*) and is more likely to use words of Latin origin (e.g. *assist* rather than *help*).

Match the formal words 1–7 with the less formal equivalents a–g, as in the example.

1 ascertain
2 commence
3 particulars
4 prior to
5 remittance
6 terminate
7 utilize

a use
b start
c payment
d find out
e end
f details
g before

3 Look at the two emails below. Which is formal and which is informal?

Look at the words and expressions in *blue italics* in the email 1 and find the equivalent expressions in email 2, as in the example.

e.g. *assistance* – help

1

I wonder if you could be of *assistance* with a problem I am having with the CD Roms I *received* with your software package. *I would be grateful if you could inform me* what *steps I should take* and any *further* information I might *require*. Also, could you *provide* me with an updated version of the manual. *Reply as soon as possible* to the above address as I urgently need to start using the software.

2

Sorry for the delay in getting back to you, but we only got your message now as our lines were down yesterday. Sorry to hear about the problems with the CDs. The attached document should be of some help – please let me know if you need any more details about what to do.

Re the updated manual – I'll get back to you asap (it's currently at the press) but I could send you a pdf file of the manual if this would help.

4 Now choose one of the emails to rewrite in either a more or a less formal tone.

5 Look at the email messages on top of page 35. The first sender wanted to write an informal message, and the second a formal message. Underline any expressions with the wrong level of formality, and rewrite them in a more appropriate way.

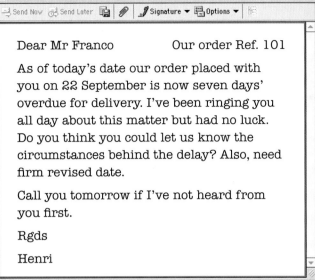

Hi John,

How are things? I was wondering if you could help me with a problem I've been having with your software. As I informed you at our meeting of 10 March, the system crashes whenever I utilize the Index option. Could you possibly provide me with a debugged version of the software.

Thank you in advance for your help.

With kind regards

Willy

Dear Mr Franco   Our order Ref. 101

As of today's date our order placed with you on 22 September is now seven days' overdue for delivery. I've been ringing you all day about this matter but had no luck. Do you think you could let us know the circumstances behind the delay? Also, need firm revised date.

Call you tomorrow if I've not heard from you first.

Rgds

Henri

 **6** Read the tips below, then choose two of the following situations to write an email for. Make sure you use the appropriate level of formality.

1 A request to know the status of an order (computer ordered 8 September, ref. no. ZY2946, six phone calls no success).

2 A message to say that the documents are on their way in the post (contract sent yesterday, needs signing, deadline for return next Thursday).

3 A complaint about not receiving a reply to an email (sent request for info re training course on 7 last month).

4 An apology to a good friend whose birthday you forgot (birthday last week, very busy at work so completely forgot, suggest meeting next week).

CYBERTIP

Choosing the appropriate level of formality

+ When deciding what register (level of formality) to use, take into account how formal other cultures may be (e.g. USA often informal, Asia often formal).

+ If you are making first contact, it is better to be quite formal.

+ If you are replying, it is a good idea to match your correspondent's level of formality. If they sign themselves *Regards, Henri* you can write *Dear Henri* in your reply. If they write *Regards Henri Penn*, you may decide to reply *Dear Henri Penn* or *Dear Mr Penn*.

+ When you have chosen an appropriate level of formality, make sure the whole email (not just parts of it!) is written at such a level.

+ You may decide to be less formal when you get to know your correspondent better.

+ Informal words tend to be shorter than their formal equivalents e.g. *try / attempt, have / possess*. Phrasal verbs are also generally less formal, e.g. *go in / enter, carry out / perform*.

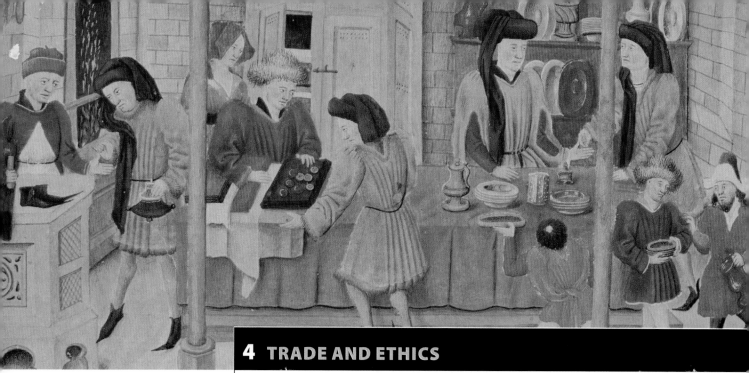

4 TRADE AND ETHICS

KICK OFF

1 Look at the picture. What is happening?

2 Discuss these questions.

1 How many of the items you have worn, used, eaten, and drunk today come from another country? Compare with a partner.

2 What do you understand by 'globalization'? How has it affected you as a consumer?

WORDS AT WORK

Globalization

3 The texts below are from a book about globalization and how it affects businesses. Read them through quickly. Which one is:

a in favour of globalization **b** neutral **c** against globalization?

1

How noble is global?

Globalization of the economy has brought immense benefits to advanced countries, such as the UK, and has encouraged growth and development in many Asian and Latin American countries, though Africa is not yet one of its beneficiaries. One of the benefits of globalization is the widespread connecting of people, sharing of information and ideas brought about in part by the Internet. 160 million people are now connected to email. 400 million people now travel each year to another continent, admittedly at great cost to the environment – one passenger journey produces as much pollution as a family car in one year.

transnational (*n*) – a company which operates in / between many countries and isn't based in one
GNP – gross national product – total value of goods and services produced by a country
turnover (*n*) – total amount of products and services sold by a company
wage (*n*) – money you earn for work (salary)
plough back (*v*) – to put the profits back into a business to improve it

2

An entire global industry can be dominated by a small number of companies. For example, 85% of global tea trade is controlled by just a few companies. An entire country can depend on a single transnational company. Transnationals provide only 5% of employment whilst controlling 70% of world trade. 51% of the top economic units in the world are now companies not countries. It is argued that such companies are not intrinsically interested in the countries in which they operate as employers and they have been accused of abusing their power. Often they adopt lower health and safety standards and employ workers in countries with the lowest wages and plough most of the profits and taxes back home.

3

As an indication of the size and importance, the turnover of four of the biggest transnationals, General Motors, Ford, Exxon, Shell exceeds that of the whole of Africa. Microsoft has optimized its operations to the extent that it is now larger than many national economies (e.g. Switzerland). Twenty-five years ago there were 7,000 transnationals; today there are 40,000. 90% are in the industrialized world. The top 500 companies control 7% of world trade, 80% of foreign investment and 30% of GNP. The combined turnover of the ten largest transnationals exceeds the GNP of a large group of Third World countries.

Global Forces

2 Complete the following using appropriate words from the texts. You will sometimes have to change the form of the word, as in the example.

The effect of globalization are:

1 People _communicate_ more with each other across the globe.
2 The economy of many Asian and Latin American countries has g_____ and d_____ .
3 The Internet and email mean that people can sh_____ ideas and knowledge.
4 Tr_____ between continents is much more widespread.
5 A few small companies can d_____ an entire global industry.
6 The environment suffers from the p_____ caused by the great increase in air travel.
7 In some cases, small countries can d_____ too heavily on a single transnational company.
8 Global companies can ab_____ their economic power by failing to pl_____ b_____ their profits into the economies of the countries in which they operate.

3 Which sentences in **2** are about the advantages of globalization and which about the disadvantages? Label each sentence A (advantage), or B (disadvantage).

Can you think of any other advantages and disadvantages?

World trade is 17 times greater than 50 years ago. But over that period Latin America's share of world trade has fallen from 11% to 5% and Africa's from 8% to 2%. The 20% of people at the top end of the global incomes scale today earn 86 times more than the 20% at the lower end. In 1997 the figure was 74; in the 1960s it was 30.

(((4.1)))

Guardian Weekly

4 Complete the table below, as in the example. You will find most, but not all, of the words in the texts.

noun	adjective	verb
economy	*economic*[1]	*economize* [5]
industry	_____ [2]	_____ [6]
globe	_____ [3]	_____ [7]
nation	_____ [4]	_____ [8]

Mark the correct stress pattern for each of the words, as in the example. Then listen and check your answers.

5 Now complete this table with the noun forms of the verbs and mark the stress. The stress falls on the same syllable for all the nouns. Which one?

verb	noun
dominate	
indicate	
communicate	
operate	
inform	
optimize	

(((4.2))) Now listen and check your answers.

6 Ask and answer the questions with a partner.

1 How much attention do you pay to how your country's economy is going? What are the main economic problems at the moment?
2 Do you think your country's economy benefits from globalization?
3 What effect does globalization have on your company?

THE INTERVIEW

The Fairtrade Foundation

Name: Julia Powell
Position: Head of Communications
Company: Fairtrade
Field of Business: Licensing UK companies to use the Fairtrade mark
Head Office: London, UK

1 Think of three foods that you buy regularly which are grown in your own country and three that are not. Are the imported foods relatively more or less expensive? Which countries do you think they come from?

2 The Fairtrade Foundation (UK) helps producers in developing countries. Read the text below, taken from the Fairtrade website, and find:

1 three reasons why farmers in developing countries make so little profit.
2 two ways in which Fairtrade helps them.

commodity (n) – product that can you can buy and sell
crop (n) – plant grown in large quantities especially for food
fertilizer (n) – chemicals that make plants grow better
pesticide (n) – chemical used to kill insects that attack crops

Address [   ] → go

Fairtrade: a better deal for developing countries

Many of the products that people in the Northern hemisphere depend on – such as coffee, tea, and chocolate – are produced in the warmer climates of the South. The prices consumers pay for these commodities have not risen in real terms over the last 40 years; but the value of fertilizers, pesticides, machinery and equipment (imported from richer countries) has increased substantially. On top of this, the market price of commodities frequently drops below the cost of producing them.

As a result of this imbalance, many of the people who grow these crops now have to work harder and longer for less money. They are often isolated, and not in a position to negotiate when selling their produce.

The Fairtrade Foundation was set up in recognition of the important role that consumers could play in improving the situation for producers. The Foundation licenses companies in the UK to put the Fairtrade Mark on products which they have bought the raw materials for directly from farmers' organizations at guaranteed prices and on fair terms. It aims to strengthen farmers' organizations and help them get into the market through the companies it licenses.

(((4.3)))

3 Listen to the interview with Julia Powell and choose the correct answer(s) to the questions below. In some cases there is more than one answer.

1 Which of these crops does Julia mention?
  a coffee   **b** tea   **c** sugar   **d** cocoa   **e** rice
2 How many farmers is she talking about in total?
  a 6 million   **b** 7 million   **c** 11 million   **d** 17 million
3 Which of these areas does she mention?
  a Latin America   **b** Africa   **c** Indonesia   **d** China
4 Who are the farmers dependent on to sell their coffee?
  a local dealers   **b** machinery vendors   **c** exporters

5 Why are farmers not in a good position to bargain for a good price?

   a they can't speak English   **b** they don't know the market price
   c they lack machinery and transport

6 Which of the following are true? Local farmers' associations:

   a are democratic   **b** control the world coffee price
   c help farmers take control of the export process

7 Which of the following statements about the world price of coffee are true?

   a it is very low   **b** it fluctuates dramatically
   c it is sometimes less than the price of production

8 What does Fairtrade's minimum price cover?

   a production costs   **b** repairs to machinery   **c** basic living wage

Listening tip

(((4.4))) ④

In spoken English, the pronunciation of a word changes according to whether it is stressed or unstressed. The unstressed form of a word is known as its 'weak form'. The following are often unstressed:

auxiliary verbs, e.g. *have, was*	prepositions, e.g. *for, to, from*
conjunctions, e.g. *and, because*	definers, e.g. *a, the, some*

You will hear each of the sentences below twice. Notice the difference between the strong (stressed) and the weak (unstressed) forms of *have, and,* and *was*. How are the pairs of sentences different in meaning?

1 You have been to Nicaragua before haven't you?
2 They're selling coffee and tea.
3 She was there at 9 o' clock.

(((4.5))) ⑤

Read and listen to two more extracts. In **1**, Julia describes a farmer's problems; in **2**, how Fairtrade has improved his life. For each of the pairs 1–15 underline which words you hear.

I *have / had*¹ met a few coffee farmers in different countries, and one farmer, *a / one*² man called Mario Pérez, has *been / was*³ telling me that only a couple of years before he felt like he had to practically give away his coffee *as / because*⁴ what he *is / was*⁵ earning *for / from*⁶ it wasn't enough to cover the costs that he *had / has*⁷ incurred in growing it. ...

1

… And / Then⁸ he said, 'for / it's⁹ the first time in a long time I feel proud'. They were able to start actually investing in / on¹⁰ their own families' future and been / being¹¹ able to do the kind as / of¹² things that we take for / from¹³ granted, like sending children at / to¹⁴ school equipped with notepads and / or¹⁵ pens, and being able to afford basic things like medicine. ■■■

2

⑥ ## Talking point

When buying food, how interested are you in the following? Organize the list in order of priority.

– has it been genetically modified?
– can I cook it quickly?
– is it healthy / good for me?
– the producer's ethical reputation
– country of origin
– price
– is it fattening?
– has it been grown organically?
– is the packaging attractive?
– quality

GRAMMAR AT WORK

Countable and uncountable nouns, quantifiers

1 Countable nouns can be either singular or plural.
*The **price** of coffee is dictated by fluctuations in stock exchanges.*
Coffee prices are now low.

2 Uncountable nouns can't be plural and can't be used with 'a' or 'one'
*Third world farmers have no money to buy any **machinery**.*
You can't say 'a machinery' or 'machineries'. You say:
*He needs two new **pieces of** machinery.*

3 Some nouns have both countable and uncountable uses with a difference in meaning.
*They trade in **coffee**. (the substance / commodity)*
*I'd like **a coffee** please. (a cup of coffee)*
*I'd like some writing **paper**. (the commodity)*
*He's going out to buy a **paper**. (a newspaper)*

▶ **For more on countable and uncountable nouns, see the Reference section page 118.**

❶ Underline the countable nouns and circle the uncountable nouns in the text below. Which uncountable nouns can also be countable units, if used with 'a piece of'?

e.g. *some coal* (uncountable), *pieces of coal* (countable)

By 1900, Britain had gained considerable experience in manufacturing and her main exports were dominated by textiles, coal, and steel. The main imports were grain, flour, meat, raw cotton, and wood (for paper). Today, the main fields of business are cars, which are both the biggest imports and exports, followed by office machinery and electrical machinery.

❷ Look at the list of nouns in the margin that are usually uncountable in English (i.e. you can't say '*an advice*' or '*two damages*'). Which ones would be countable in your language?

advice
damage
equipment
evidence
feedback
furniture
information
luggage
money
news
progress
research
software
traffic
work

❸ Underline the correct form or forms (see Reference section p118 for help). Then ask and answer the questions with a partner.

1 Have you read the newspaper today? *Is / Are* there any interesting news?

2 Money *doesn't / don't* equal happiness – do you agree?

3 How *much / many* product and market *research / researches* does your company do?

4 Is there *a lot of / lots of / many* traffic in your town? Why? How *much / many* is being done to reduce it?

5 How *much / many* customers or suppliers do you personally deal with? Do you get *much feedback / many feedbacks* about your products and services from them?

6 *A little knowledge / few knowledges* about everything is better than *a lot of / several* knowledge about a *little / few* things – do you agree?

BUSINESS SKILLS

Running meetings, expressing opinions

1 Answer the questions and compare answers with a partner.

1 How many meetings do you go to in a month?
2 Are they formal or informal?
3 What are they for? (e.g. team meetings, project updates, etc.)
4 Are they always necessary?
5 What would you like to change about them?

2 Now look at the tips for effective meetings. In what ways do the meetings you attend follow this model, and how are they different?

ESSENTIAL **DK** MANAGERS

MANAGING MEETINGS

CHAIRING·AIMS
CONTRIBUTING
PROCEDURES·NOTE-TAKING
DYNAMICS   VENUES
CONSENSUS   PACING
SEATING·GOALS
AGENDAS·TASKS

TIPS FOR EFFECTIVE MEETINGS

1 The meeting is arranged for the best day and time; its purpose is clear.

2 The right people and the right number of people attend.

3 The chairperson opens the meeting on time and explains its purpose.

4 Items on the agenda are discussed in turn and within a pre-established time limit.

5 The chairperson ensures attendees contribute in a relevant and positive way.

6 Options are explored, compromise is negotiated, and decisions reached.

7 The chairperson checks agreement and summarizes main points.

8 The meeting ends on time and there is a follow up (e.g. email summarizing decisions, minutes).

(((4.6))) **3** You are going to hear extracts from a meeting. Listen and match the extracts 1–5 with the meeting stage *a–e* each comes from, as in the example.

a starting the meeting
b moving on to the next item
c getting other people's opinions

d summarizing (
e ending the meeting

4 Listen again and complete the sentences.

a starting	**b** moving on	**c** getting opinions	**d** summarizing	**e** ending

OK. _____ everyone's here now. _____ started?	Excellent, so _____ _____ _____ the next item now.	OK but _____ _____ think? María Jesus, _____ it?	OK, let's _____ _____ what we've decided.	Well I think _____ . _____ Thank you all for _____ .

5 How strongly do you agree that the following are acceptable?

completely   partially   not sure   disagree

← ——→

a investing in shares of a company that infringes human rights
b occasionally adding personal expenses to your business expenses
c occasionally taking sick leave when you are well
d giving gifts to current and potential customers
e taking stationery (pens, paper, etc.) from work for personal use at home

6 Do the expressions below indicate agreement (A) or disagreement (D)?

1 *That's true, but …*
2 *I see what you're saying.*
3 *I don't think so.*
4 *Absolutely. / Precisely. / Exactly.*

5 *I'm not so sure about that.*
6 *That's beside the point.*
7 *Yes, however it seems to me that …*
8 *You've got a point there.*

(((4.7)))
7 Now listen to some people discussing the issues in **5**. Which expressions from **6** do they use? Which two issues do the speakers discuss?

8 How important is it for a company to be ethical? Read the passage below about an official list of ethical businesses.

rated (*adj*) – given a mark or score for sth
enable (*v*) – to make it possible
comply with (*v*) – to obey a rule / order, etc.
adhere to (*v*) – to behave according to a rule / law, etc.
controversial (*adj*) – causes a lot of angry discussion / disagreement

The FTSE (Financial Times Stock Exchange) in London has an index of companies (FTSE 4 Good) which have been rated for their principles of social responsibility. This enables anyone interested in investing money, to choose a company which complies with their sense of what is ethical.

A perfect company would be one that has very good environmental policies, has looked at human rights issues around the world, and ensures their company adheres to it. It would probably operate in a sector not considered controversial.

9 Work in small groups. You are part of the FTSE 4 Good index committee and are meeting to decide which companies to include on the new index.

1 Elect a chairperson whose job is to ensure that the meeting follows points 3–8 in the effective meeting tips. Decide which sectors of industry below you would automatically exclude from the index and why.
2 For each of the remaining sectors, brainstorm to think of two or three well-known companies.
3 Decide which of these companies you would include in the index and why. Are there any companies in these sectors you would exclude?

In the United States today, consumers and consumer activists boycott over 800 products.
http://exchanges.state

| banking | clothing | tobacco | information technology | pharmaceuticals |
| food | media | petroleum | car manufacturing | |

EXTENDED SPEAKING

Planning an induction day

1 Discuss these questions.

1 During your first days at work, what information did you need to know about your new company – e.g. rules and regulations, training courses available, union representation, overtime policy?

2 Did you have any induction events or training?

3 If you did have an induction event, what happened? How useful was it? If you didn't, do you think it would have been useful to have one?

2 Your company is expanding rapidly. The company is planning an induction day in which approximately 50 employees will have an opportunity to get to know each other and are given a general introduction to the company. The event must be fun as well as informative.

Look at the following information:

To: Induction Day Organizers

From: Levi Potak, Facilities Manager

Re: Facilities for the induction day:
Monday 5 April 9.00 a.m.–5.00 p.m.

The Main Common Room is available all morning and from 3:00 p.m. in the afternoon. Unfortunately it is booked for a sales presentation between 1:00 and 2:30. Since it is the only meeting room with Powerpoint, this cannot be changed. The Green Room (capacity 30) is available from 12:00 onwards. The Jackson Room (capacity 30) is available all day.

Notes from training seminar

Possible types of activity for an induction day:

- formal presentations - Powerpoint, overhead projector and transparencies, videos
- informal talks followed by discussion groups
- role plays and simulations
- icebreakers - short activities to allow as many people as possible to get to know each other
- games and competitions

Re: availability of senior staff to give presentations for the induction day

I have contacted the individuals concerned as requested and asked about availability on the induction day on Monday 5 April. The response was as follows:

Richard Herrera, the CEO, is only available after 3.00 p.m.

Elisabeta Finkelstein, the Human Resources Manager, will be free from 1.00 p.m. onwards.

It will only be possible to get representatives for all the Heads of Department if we ask them to come right at the beginning of the day.

Representatives from the SUMCO and APT, the two trade unions, have to come in their own time, so could only come in the lunch period between 12.00 and 2.00.

I hope this helps!

Karina Lee

Human Resources Assistant

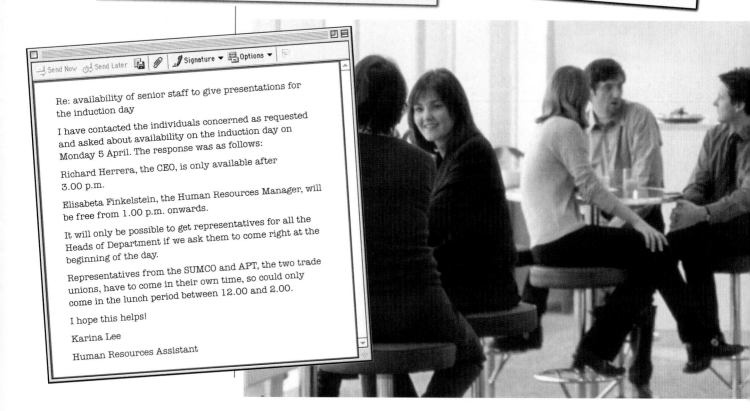

3 Work in small groups.

1 Decide on the programme of events for the induction day, and produce a schedule. This should include:
- what each person is going to talk about (think about what the employees most want to know).
- how they are going to present the information and what they are going to need in terms of equipment, etc.
- when these events are going to happen on the schedule and which rooms you are going to use.
- when the breaks are going to happen on the schedule. What sort of food / drink are you going to provide?

2 Decide who on your team will be responsible for organizing what – e.g. Who will introduce the speakers? Who will organize the necessary equipment?

3 Try and make the programme of events as lively and varied as possible.

4 Each team has to present their schedule of activities to the whole class.

1 Decide who is going to be responsible for talking about which aspects of the schedule. Everyone in the team must speak.
2 Put together a presentation, using some visual aids if possible.
3 Take it in turns to try and sell your group's plan for the day to the whole class.

WORDS AT WORK

Link words and connectors

a

b

c

d

1 Look at the genuine inventions illustrated in the pictures above.

1 Can you identify what each one is and what it would be used for?
2 Do you think there is a potential market for these products in your country? why/why not?

2 Read through the texts quickly. Which product(s) from **1** does each of the texts talk about?

3 Only one of the inventions had short-term success. Which one was it? Why did all the others fail?

1

to trigger (*v*) – to start or activate sth suddenly
to fade (*v*) – to disappear slowly
fad (*n*) – sth that people are interested in for a short time

1

The Scott Paper Company in the US **triggered an international mania** for paper clothes when it offered paper dresses by mail order. Within six months Scott had sold more than half a million of the dresses. There were paper bikinis and paper vacation clothes – you travelled without luggage, bought your clothes at the vacation site, and threw them away when you got home. *Although*[1] *Time* magazine noted that paper clothing was **'here to stay'**, paper clothing **turned out to be a fast fading fad**. *In fact*[2] , designers didn't really like paper *since*[3] it was hard to work with and obviously didn't last.

2

to invent (*v*) – to produce or design sth that has not existed before
invention (*n*) – a thing or idea which a person has invented
patent (*n*) – the official right to be the only person to use or sell a new invention
to patent (*n*) – to get or obtain patent
take up (*v*) – to use
impracticality (*n*) – from *impractical* (*adj*)– very difficult to use in real life

2

Between 1962 and 1977 an Englishman, Arthur Pedrick, patented 162 inventions. *Even though*[4] his ideas were extremely creative, none of them were **taken up commercially** *due to*[5] their impracticality and non-utility. His inventions included a bicycle with amphibious capacity (*i.e.*[6] for use on land or water), and a way to enable people to drive a car from the back seat. *However*[7] his greatest invention was a means to irrigate deserts by sending a constant supply of snowballs from the Polar regions through a network of giant pea-shooters.

④ Can you understand the meaning of the expressions in **bold** from the context? Try to paraphrase them (find another way of saying the same thing). Compare your ideas with a partner.

⑤ The words 1–7 in *blue italics* are connectors or link words and they help the authors to organize the text by linking ideas together. Match the link words with their meanings *a–f* below, as in the example.

▶ For more on link words see the Reference section page 122.

a but ⑦
b that is
c because of

d despite the fact that (2 words)
e in reality
f because

⑥ Now read the text below about the videophone and circle the most appropriate link words / expressions, as in the example.

3

Shortly after launching the 'see-as-you-talk phone' at the 1964 New York World Fair, AT&T made the revolutionary service available in New York, Chicago, and Washington DC. There were high hopes for the innovation, *but /(despite)/ yet*[1] the obvious drawbacks, *e.g. / i.e.*[2] the picturephone calls cost twenty times as much as an ordinary call, arrangements to use the new technology had to be made in advance by regular phone, and customers had to go to a special location to have a conversation.

By 1970, it had an improved version of the picturephone technology ready. There were projections of the sale or lease of a hundred thousand phones in five years, with the prediction that phones with pictures would be 'widely used by the general public' by the 1980s. Again, *consequently / due to / since*[3] its poor performance, the market place put the picturephone on hold.

The 'break-through' system used in 1992's version, VideoPhone 2500, was faster than older models, *because / but / therefore*[4] its picture quality was much inferior to the full motion video and synchronized audio of television. *Even though / However / Thus*[5] once again the picturephone didn't meet projections. As *a consequence of / Despite / In reality*[6] these failures, the technology continues to move ahead.

GRAMMAR AT WORK

Future predictions

We can use a variety of forms to predict the future:

will + infinitive: *Marriage* **will become** *more common.*
going to + infinitive: *Look out! Your laptop* **is going to** *fall off your desk.*
might + infinitive: *Videophones* **might** *soon be a reality.*
could + infinitive: *This kind of marketing* **could** *lead to an increase in junk mail.*

Complete the rules in the box below.

---

1 *Could* and _____ are used when we do not feel certain about what we are predicting.
2 *Going to* and *will* can be used to make predictions when we are more certain. Often there is little difference in meaning.
3 _____ is used when there is concrete or visible evidence that something is about to happen.
4 _____ refers to the way we more personally see the future.

▶ **For more on future predictions, see the Reference section page 120.**

---

❶ Make some predictions about your situation in five years' time in the following areas. Discuss them with a partner.

– work: type of job, level of responsibility, amount of travel, working hours
– family and free time: marital status, children, how you spend time at the weekends / on holiday
– where you live: rented, owned, house, flat, town, region, country

❷ Write a short report predicting your company's situation in five years' time. Try to connect your ideas using the appropriate connectors and linking expressions from the *Words at work* section.

– size
– location
– diversity of products
– overseas markets

– brand development
– corporate image
– profits
– market share

Future plans and decisions

(((5.4))) **❸** Look at the list of functions 1–8. Listen to eight extracts from conversations and circle the tense that the speaker uses (or mainly uses) for the function as in the example. W= *will*, GT = *going to*, PC = *present continuous*

1	making spontaneous decisions on the phone	W	GT
2	introducing a presentation	(W)	GT
3	offering to help a colleague do something (2nd speaker)	W	GT
4	ordering food in a restaurant	W	GT
5	reporting arrangements made at an earlier time	PC	GT
6	summarizing decisions taken in a meeting	PC	GT
7	asking about a colleague's travel (or holiday, weekend) plans	PC	W
8	talking about a strong intention made at an earlier time	GT	W

4 Look at the tenses you have circled in ❶. Which tense do we use:

1 to make a decision or offer spontaneously (at the moment of speaking)?
2 to talk about decisions or arrangements that have already been made?
3 to talk about intentions, when perhaps no real plans have been made yet?

▶ **For more on future plans and decisions, see the Reference section page 120.**

5 How far ahead do you generally make plans for the future in terms of:

– work   – social life   – holidays?

With your partner, discuss your plans for:

– this evening   – this weekend   – next week   – your next holiday

6 Work with a different partner and exchange information about your company's plans for the future. (If you are from the same company discuss your own particular department or project.) Talk about:

– expanding into new markets
– launching new products
– improving existing products
– saving money

– taking on / laying off staff
– researching new projects
– investing in machinery / equipment

People are spending less time eating lunch. More than half (56%) of American workers take 15 minutes or less for lunch. The average lunch takes 29 minutes. 63% miss lunch completely once or twice a week. 20% have no lunch three to five times a week.

Business Life

BUSINESS SKILLS

Business socializing

1 Read the following tips about business socializing in two different countries. Which is the most similar to your own country?

1

Give yourself time to get used to the strong flavours and smells of the national cuisine. It is delicious, but the heavy use of garlic and spices can come as a shock! Learn to use chopsticks – you can only eat rice with a spoon – and kneeling at a low table to eat. All the dishes in a meal are usually served together. You have your own bowl of rice, and you take what you want from the other dishes on the table with your chopsticks. If you pick up or touch something with your chopsticks, you must take it! When passing dishes, it is good manners to support the arm that is holding the dish with your other hand. Don't start or finish eating until the most senior person has started or finished.

2

Get used to eating slowly! Come prepared for a long and convivial evening, where the company and the conversation is as important as the food. Listening to and telling anecdotes – amusing stories – is enjoyed by everyone. The meal will probably begin with a selection of salads and starters – smoked fish, caviar, and pickled vegetables are typical. These are often served with small glasses of alcohol. Toasting with this is a national tradition (the guests will all try and think of witty and amusing toasts). You make a much better impression if you try to join in, even if you only drink water! If half the guests suddenly disappear for 20 minutes half-way through the meal they have probably gone outside for a cigarette. This is quite acceptable, and it is acceptable for you to join them if you smoke yourself.

1 Try to guess which countries the tips refer to before checking with the key on page 106. How easy / difficult was it to guess? Which other countries could the tips refer to?

2 How useful do you find cultural tips like these? What are the dangers of making such generalizations?

(((5.5))) **2** Listen to the following two conversations and answer the questions.

1 Is the tone of the conversations informal or formal?

2 When do they arrange to meet?

3 What change to the original arrangements do they then make?

4 Where and at what time do they arrange to meet?

3 Look at the useful expressions for inviting and making arrangements on page 132. Which of these expressions were used in the conversations in **2**? Listen again and check your answers.

4 Work with a partner. Take it in turns to invite each other to lunch. Student A, use the information in File 7 on page 110, and Student B, look at File 15 on page 114. Use as many of the expressions from page 132 as you can.

(((5.6))) **5** On the opposite page are some typical expressions that might be used at a business lunch in a restaurant. Work with a partner and try to fill in the gaps.

Make small talk on arrival: This is a nice place, _____ here before?

Ask for/offer explanation of menu: _____ 'hotpot?'

Make suggestion/recommendation: _____, it's really good.

Order from the menu: OK _____ one fish and chips and one hotpot. And could we also _____ still mineral water?

Check guest is happy: Did you _____ your hotpot?

Show appreciation: Yes it was _____.

Offer to order something else: Now _____ a dessert?

Decline offer: No _____. The hotpot was very filling.

Accept offer: Yes _____ nice, thanks.

Offer to pay: Now I _____ for this. It's _____ me.

Thank the host/guest: Well _____ very much, that's very _____ of you.

Listen to a conversation in a restaurant and check your answers.

⑥ Work with a partner. Roleplay the story illustrated in the pictures. Use as much of the language from ❸ and ❺ as you can.

EMAIL

Making and clarifying arrangements

1 Discuss the questions below.

1 What kind of arrangements do you have to make in your job, e.g. for meetings, lunches, travel?

2 Is it easier to make such arrangements by phone or by email? What are the advantages and disadvantages of each method?

2 You are organizing a work dinner for yourself and a senior colleague. Write an email to him / her with the following details.

1 Give a reason for the dinner.

2 Suggest a place, day, and time.

3 Suggest something to do either before or after the dinner.

4 Ask for a quick reply.

3 Exchange your emails with a partner and write brief replies.

1 Thank the sender for the invitation.

2 Acknowledge the reason for the dinner.

3 Agree on the place and time, but suggest another day.

4 Say you are unable to do anything either before or after the dinner, and give a reason.

4 You want to write an email to confirm the arrangements for a meeting with a customer, Umesh Patel. Look at the notes below and complete the email. Give him your mobile phone number and ask for his. End the email in an appropriate way.

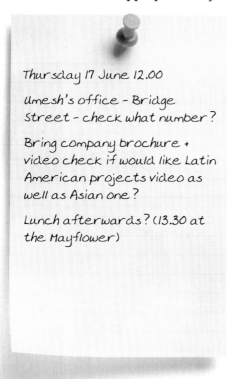

Thursday 17 June 12.00

Umesh's office - Bridge Street - check what number?

Bring company brochure + video check if would like Latin American projects video as well as Asian one?

Lunch afterwards? (13.30 at the Mayflower)

Dear Umesh

It was good to speak to you. I just wanted to check the details of our arrangements. So, we're meeting on …

5 Sometimes emails are so concise or are written so quickly that the meaning is not clear. In such cases you may need to ask for clarification.

Write replies to the two emails below. The information that you need to ask for / clarify is in brackets. See the example below.

1

Carrie

Yes, certainly. *[referring to?]*

Another thing, I am afraid the meeting has been put off till Thursday *[this week? same time? same place?]*. In the meantime I can tell you that the contractors have estimated that the cost will be in the region of 100,000 *[$? £?]*. The name of the senior contractor is Andrea *[male or female?]* Cavalieri, just in case you want to make contact.

That's all for now.

Jo

Jo

I'm not sure what your 'yes' was referring to; could you clarify?

Just a couple of other things I want to clear up: …

2

Dear Mr Peters

I am writing to confirm the arrangements for your visit to Beijing next week. You will be arriving on Monday at 05.00 at Beijing *[meet at airport?]* and departing Sunday at 10.30.

The meeting with our lawyers will be at our offices *[where? time?]*. Mr Chang *[who?]* will also be attending.

There will be a dinner in your honour on Sunday evening *[mistake? leaving Sunday morning]* which we would be very pleased if you could attend *[bring wife?]*.

With our very best wishes.

Ms Tau Pei Lin

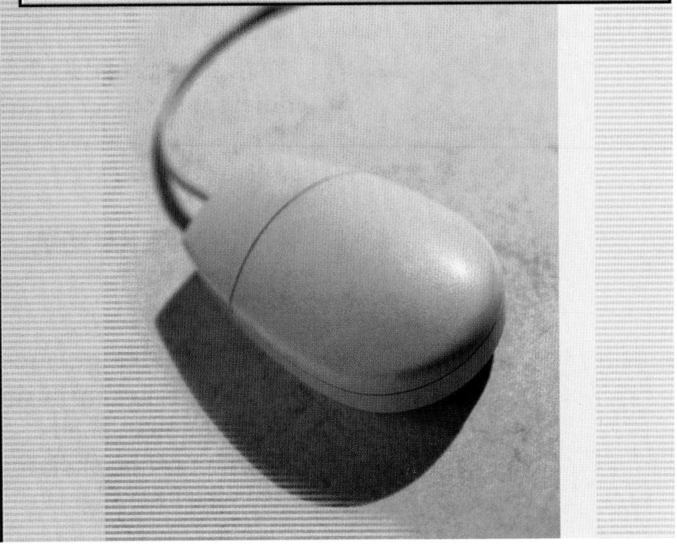

6 You have 30 seconds to write each of the email messages below. When you have finished, pass them to your partner who will try to improve them by making them more concise and / or clearer.

1 Inform a colleague that you cannot attend the meeting tomorrow. You want them to phone you about it later.

2 You want to arrange a meeting as soon as possible with an important client about a problem that has recently come up to do with an order. You are free any afternoon next week apart from Friday.

6 COMMUNICATION

Sistine Chapel Ceiling: Creation of Adam, detail of the outstretched arms, 1510 (fresco) (post-restoration) by Michelangelo Buonarroti (1475–1564) Vatican Museums and Galleries, Vatican City, Italy/Bridgeman Art Library

KICK OFF

1 Look at the painting. What does it show? How do people communicate today?

2 Do you ever experience communication problems in dealing with colleagues from abroad? If so, how do they arise and how do you handle them?

3 What aspects of daily life or culture have you found surprising and different in other countries you have had contact with?

THE INTERVIEW

Babel

Babel is a training company which aims to help business people improve their communication skills for dealing with overseas clients.

Name:	Sue Hyde
Position:	Business Development Manager
Company:	Babel Language and Cultural Consultants
Field of Business:	Cultural training
Head Office:	UK

(((6.1))) **1** Listen to Sue Hyde and tick (✓) the points below that she mentions.

- ☐ saying 'please'
- ☐ formality
- ☐ shaking hands
- ☐ kissing
- ☐ anger
- ☐ names
- ☐ table manners
- ☐ eye contact

2 Listen again – and answer the questions.

1 What example does Sue give of something important in British culture?
2 What does she say about names?
3 What three specific pieces of advice does she give about gifts?

3 Compare ideas with a partner. What advice do you think Babel gave the people below? What advice would you give?

1
A **British** man was regularly sent out to Milan in Italy on behalf of a pharmaceutical company to secure a contract with an Italian company. His trips were always brief and to the point; he went straight to Milan and flew back in the same day and yet he never managed to clinch the deal.

2
A **Chinese** man had been working in Britain for 20 years. Even though his English was good he wasn't able to do presentations which he felt was stopping him from getting ahead in the company. His presentations tended to be very long and people had difficulty in following them.

3
A **Dutch** woman had done a PhD in Britain in Economics and was working for an investment company also in the UK. Her problem was that even though her English was good, she found it difficult to contribute in meetings. People assumed that because she didn't say anything she didn't understand.

4
A **French** woman kept receiving emails from her British counterpart asking for clarification of a certain point. The French woman rang her to explain the situation but was puzzled to receive several further emails over the next few days repeating the request for written clarification. The French woman became annoyed with her counterpart's insistence and her British counterpart decided the French woman was inefficient.

(((6.2))) **4** Now listen to Sue explaining what happened. Write a brief summary of each case – compare Babel's advice with your own solutions.

Listening tip

(((6.3))) **5** Some pairs of words have similar pronunciation but different spelling, e.g. *were / sir*. In other cases, the spelling is the same but the sound is different. e.g. *there / here*.

1 Listen and compare: **a** *were / sir* with **b** *there / here*
2 Circle the words with the same vowel sound as the word in **bold.**

(/ɜː/) **were**	where, work, fork, world, learn, year, terms director, first, thirty
(/ɔː/) **brought**	taught, your, courses, because, launch, colour, walk
(/ɪə/) **hear**	we're, wear, clearly, teach, really, deal, between
(/ɑː/) **part**	our, tour, are, share, particular, market

(((6.4))) **6** Listen and check your answers to **2**. Then add two more words with the same vowel sound to each list and compare with your partner.

7 ## Talking point

What cultural tips would you give for your country regarding: alcohol, smoking, religion, status of women and acceptable topics of conversation?

WORDS AT WORK

Verbs with prepositions

1 Complete the table, then compare results with your partner.

	your current situation	your ideal
days of holiday per year		
working hours per week		
working days per week		
minutes for lunch break		
hours of overtime per week		
hours of travelling / commuting per week		
acceptable time late for business appointments		

2 Read the texts below and underline the facts that you find the most interesting or surprising. Then compare with your partner.

3 Look at the expressions in blue in text 1.

1 Note which verbs and prepositions are used together.

1 HOW TO BE LATE

When do you need to *apologize for* being late? According to a book on business etiquette around the world, in Britain and North America it is acceptable to *be* five minutes *late for* a business appointment (e.g. to *take part in* a meeting, to attend a presentation). On the other hand in Britain it is not impolite to be five to 15 minutes late for a invitation to dinner. *Depending on* the importance of the dinner, people from other cultures may arrive considerably later or even not at all – as the acceptance was only to *prevent* the host *from* losing face.

2 WORKING 9–5?

In Europe actual average working week hours vary from 42.2 hours in Greece to 37.9 in Sweden. This contrasts with what European governments have actually agreed with trade unions for working hours. For example the average working week for full-time workers in France in theory should be 35 hours. In reality however, it's just under 40. Interestingly, although one of the reasons for the 35 hour week in France was to increase employment, this hasn't happened. Despite this, 39% of French companies told researchers that they expect to let their workers have a four-day week in the near future.

2 Circle the preposition that each list of verbs below is used with, as in the example (θ = no preposition).

for / of	apologize, be late, vote, wait
(at) / in	invest, participate, be interested, be included
of / with	agree, be satisfied, comply
from / on	comment, depend, focus, work
to / θ	tell, phone, call, ring, answer
to / θ	reply, say, talk, write

❹ Complete the sentences with one of the verb and preposition combinations from **❸**. Then ask and answer the questions with a partner.

1 How soon do you _____ emails after you have received them?

2 How much of your working time do you _____ 'networking' – trying to meet and talk to the right people?

3 Would you _____ being late if you arrived 10 minutes after a business dinner had begun?

4 When a friend _____ you on the phone at work, how short do you keep the conversation?

5 Do you always do what your boss _____ you to do? Why (not)?

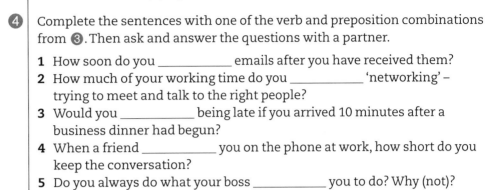

3 WORKING 8 DAYS A WEEK

The average working week in the US has increased by four hours in the last 30 years to over 45 hours. In extreme cases people have died as a result of working too long hours. The Japanese have a special name for it – karoshi. In one recorded case a man did not have one day off work, or even dinner with his family for seventeen months. He only slept between 30 minutes and two-and-a-half hours a night, and by the time he killed himself he was working until 6.30 a.m. once every three days.

4 ALL WORK AND NO PLAY

75% of US managers, compared to 2.3% of UK managers, regard leisure time as a refreshing break which will enable them to work better afterwards. Although they enjoy spending time with their family, the average American father only spends 17 minutes a day with his children. More than half American workers take 15 minutes or less for lunch, though health experts recommend taking much longer breaks.

GRAMMAR AT WORK

Verb patterns: the gerund

We use the gerund or *ing* form of the verb:

1 after a preposition,
  e.g. *I am good at* **selling**. *You use it for* **calculating**. *Before* **going** *out, I always …*
2 the subject of a sentence,
  e.g. **Walking** *is good for you.* **Paying** *taxes is obligatory.* **Smoking** *is bad for your health.*
3 after certain verbs,
  e.g. verbs describing emotional attitudes: *like, love, enjoy, hate, stand, mind.*
  verbs connected with stopping and starting: *stop, start, begin, finish, give up.*
  others: *spend, risk, avoid.*

▶ **For more on verbs with gerund and infinitive, see the Reference section page 121.**

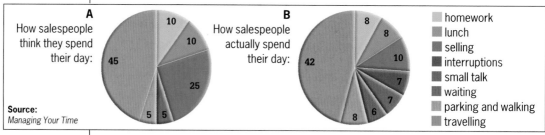

A How salespeople think they spend their day:

10, 10, 45, 25, 5, 5

B How salespeople actually spend their day:

8, 8, 10, 7, 7, 6, 8, 42

- homework
- lunch
- selling
- interruptions
- small talk
- waiting
- parking and walking
- travelling

Source: *Managing Your Time*

 1 Look at the charts above.

1 In which areas of activity is there the biggest difference between what salespeople really do and what they think they do?
2 Draw two pie charts to show:
  a how you spend your time at work
  b how you spend your time at home.

2 Compare your charts with a partner. Then discuss which activities you:

a love doing
b don't mind doing
c would like to spend more / less time doing
d would like to avoid doing completely
e have given up doing
f can't stand doing.

e.g. When I'm at home I love cooking. At work, well, I love going to meetings and getting positive feedback from satisfied customers.

Verb patterns: *to* and the infinitive

We use *to* and the infinitive:

1 after adjectives,
  e.g. *I find it difficult* **to relax**. *It's impossible* **to work** *in here. It's better* **to be** *honest.*
2 to express a purpose or a reason,
  e.g. *I'm saving* **to buy** *a car. He's going out* **to get** *a paper. We work* **to earn** *our living.*
3 after certain verbs, particularly verbs expressing future plans / intentions,
  e.g. *want, would like, need, expect, decide, hope, plan, manage, offer, promise, refuse, try, learn, seem, forget.*

3 Look at the information below about a sales meeting. Then complete the sentences below using the expressions in the box, as in the example.

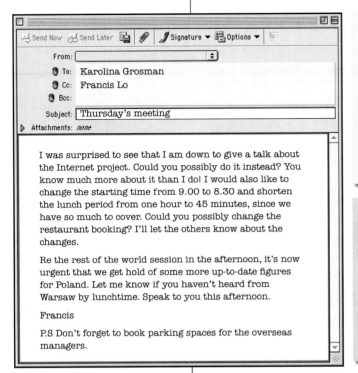

Send Now   Send Later   Signature ▼   Options ▼

From: [ ]
To: Karolina Grosman
Cc: Francis Lo
Bcc:
Subject: Thursday's meeting
Attachments: *none*

I was surprised to see that I am down to give a talk about the Internet project. Could you possibly do it instead? You know much more about it than I do! I would also like to change the starting time from 9.00 to 8.30 and shorten the lunch period from one hour to 45 minutes, since we have so much to cover. Could you possibly change the restaurant booking? I'll let the others know about the changes.

Re the rest of the world session in the afternoon, it's now urgent that we get hold of some more up-to-date figures for Poland. Let me know if you haven't heard from Warsaw by lunchtime. Speak to you this afternoon.

Francis

P.S Don't forget to book parking spaces for the overseas managers.

AGENDA FOR SALES MEETING THURS 6 MARCH

9.00	arrival and coffee
9.30 – 11.30	results and budget (*Shelby Coltrane & Francis*)
11.30 – 1.00	Internet (*Francis*)
1.00 – 2.00	lunch
2.00 – 4.00	Western Europe and the States (*each manager covers their area*)
4.00 – 5.00	rest of world (*Soon Li, anyone else?*)

> Sorry Francis – I can't do the Internet presentation – I've got too much else on! I'll give you all my notes – and any other help you need – Re the Sales figures – there's a problem with the database in Warsaw. Could you ring the Poland office asap?
> K

asks Karolina	needs	reminds Karolina	refuses	
offers	wants	~~would like Karolina~~	promises	asks Francis

1 Francis *would like Karolina* to give the talk about the Internet project in his place.
2 He _____ to change the starting time and shorten the lunch period.
3 He _____ to change the restaurant booking.
4 He _____ to let the others know about the changes.
5 He _____ to get some updated sales figures for Poland.
6 He _____ to book parking spaces for the overseas staff.
7 Karolina _____ to give the Internet project talk.
8 She _____ to help Francis prepare to give the presentation himself.
9 She _____ to ring the Poland office asap.

4 Underline the correct form of the verbs in the sentences below. Then ask and answer the questions with a partner.

1 What things are you particularly good at *to do / doing* in your job? What do you find difficult *to do / doing*?
2 What typical things does your boss **a** ask you *to do / doing*, and **b** help you *to do / doing*? **c** What do you like *to do / doing* by yourself?
3 Apart from English, what foreign language would you like *to speak / speaking* well?
4 Have you ever forgotten *to do / doing* something important at work or in your home life? What happened?
5 Where do you hope *to take / taking* your holidays this year or next year? What do you want *to do / doing* when you get there?
6 What do you think you need *to do / doing* to get a promotion?

BUSINESS SKILLS

Clarifications and explanations

① Discuss the questions in your group.

1 On what occasions do you need to communicate with your customers and suppliers? Do you prefer to communicate:
   a face-to-face   **b** by email   **c** by phone?   Why?

2 What difficulties do you associate with each form of communication?

(((6.5))) **②** Listen to this phone conversation.

1 Which one of the following are they talking about?
   a configuring a computer program
   b a client / customer survey
   c a product demonstration

2 Look at the list of expressions below and tick (✓) the expressions you remember hearing.

asking for clarification	checking listener understands
☐ Could you repeat ...?	☐ Are you with me? Is that clear?
☐ What exactly do you mean by ...?	☐ Have you got that?
☐ Sorry, I didn't get the bit about ...	**showing you've understood**
☐ A *what*, sorry?	☐ Right. That's clear.
☐ Sorry, did you say ... or	☐ OK. I'm with you.
☐ So, you're saying ...	☐ OK. I've got that.

③ Listen again and check your answers.

(((6.6))) **④** Marie rings Sharif back. Listen and write down the message.

⑤ Listen again and make a note of the expressions that the operator uses to:

1 ask Marie to speak louder.
2 check Marie's name and the name of her company.
3 check that she has understood Tuesday and not Thursday.
4 check that the extension number is sixteen and not sixty.
5 make sure she has taken down the message correctly.

⑥ Work in pairs. You are going to practise making and clarifying arrangements on the phone. Student A, look at File 6 on page 110. Student B, turn to File 14 on page 113.

7 Which of the following are you **not** able to do? Compare with a partner.

☐ configure a PC

☐ replace the toner in a printer

☐ set channels on the car radio

☐ send emails to multiple recipients

☐ load a ringing tone on to a mobile phone

☐ change electric plugs

☐ download music from the Internet

☐ send text messages on a mobile phone

☐ set the clock on a video recorder

☐ burn a CD

☐ transfer phone calls to another extension

☐ use a spreadsheet

☐ change a car wheel

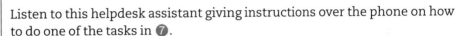

(((6.7))) **8** Listen to this helpdesk assistant giving instructions over the phone on how to do one of the tasks in **7**.

1 Which of the tasks is the assistant talking about?
2 The assistant is not helpful. What does he do or not do that makes him unhelpful?
3 How do we know the customer is having problems?

(((6.8))) **9** Now listen to another version of the conversation. Why is communication more successful this time? Write down as many reasons as you can.

10 Listen again.

1 Which of the following does the assistant do?
   a give the customer a checklist of things to do / check before starting
   b summarize each stage as he goes along
   c check at each stage that the customer is following what he says
   d give alternative descriptions of technical terms
   e give reasons why he is telling the customer to do certain things
   f pause to give the customer time to do things
2 Which of the following does the customer do?
   a check she has understood by repeating what the assistant says using different words
   b show the assistant that she has understood what she says

11 Choose one of the tasks in **7** that you know how to do.

1 Write instructions for it. Remember to talk about the typical things that can go wrong and how you can deal with them.
2 Compare your instructions with a partner. Suggest ways of improving each other's work and making it clearer.
3 Choose a new partner and give him / her the instructions. Make sure that you ask for and give clarification where necessary.

EXTENDED SPEAKING

Communication consultants

A rapidly expanding European company which sells software programs is experiencing severe communications problems.

The company has just opened offices in Sydney, Australia. The MD (Managing Director) has to spend a lot of time out of the office. He has too much work to do but is reluctant to delegate. He prefers not to waste time holding internal meetings. He has not had time to meet many of the newest members of staff. There is no formal management structure within the company.

The company is expanding rapidly and needs to recruit at least 20 new staff. The MD has previously selected all new personnel but now hasn't time. In addition the last two new recruits both resigned after two months as they felt they were not experienced enough for the posts and were not given enough training. 50% of the 40 employees are non-native speakers who have just relocated from various parts of Europe and Asia. Internal office relations are not good and staff are working under great pressure. Teams work in small groups but without knowing what other people within the company do.

Some of the non-native speakers have difficulties understanding the English of the native speakers. Clients are also getting frustrated as they often need to phone for technical help and either no-one understands the problem or no one is available to help. The MD is particularly worried about the high turnover in staff and the poor office relations.

to appoint (*v*) – to choose for a job / position of responsibility
to be reluctant (*adj*) – not want to do sth
to delegate (*v*) – to give part of your work to so else
to recruit (*v*) – to find new people to join a company
to resign (*v*) – to leave a job
frustrated (*adj*) – angry and impatient

1 Discuss these questions.

1 How much and in what ways is information shared within your company? Think about:
  a the means of sharing information
    e.g. emails, memos, meetings.
  b where information goes
    e.g. between departments, top-down (senior management to employees) and bottom-up (employees to senior management).
  c types of information,
    e.g. procedural / organizational – how systems work within the company, who is responsible for what.
    motivational / managerial – sales or production targets, contracts and orders, sales figures.
    personal – salaries, staff appointments.

2 How effective do you think your company's external communications are? Think about the company image, marketing of your products and services, etc.

2 Read the text opposite about a company's communication problems.

3 Work in small groups. You are a team in a company of consultants who specialize in improving the way companies communicate – both internally with employees and also externally with clients. Look at the following questions.

1 Which aspects of the company's problems are related to communication? Make a list of those that are not communication-related.
2 What are the main communication problems?
3 Decide which problems are the most serious and should take priority.

4 Produce the following, and decide in what form you would present each item to the company (email, presentation, etc.).

1 some general initial advice you would offer the MD
2 a short-term action plan, with suggested actions listed in order of priority
3 what types of training courses you would recommend
4 what further information you need to be able to offer long-term solutions

Camel train
GettyImages/ImageBank/Eric Meola

7 TRAVEL

KICK OFF

1 Look at the picture. Would you like to travel in this way? Why / why not?

2 Discuss these questions.

1 How much time do you personally spend 'on the road', i.e. travelling to and from the workplace or travelling as part of your job?
2 What kind of people travel for business in your company and what are the main reasons for business trips (e.g. to meet clients)?
3 Do you think business travel is likely to increase or decrease in the future?

WORDS AT WORK

Travel terms and easily confused words

1 Look at the two travellers' profiles on the opposite page. Do you travel as frequently as either of these people?

2 Read the profiles again and find words which mean:

1 bags you take on the plane with you
2 no limit on the miles in a car-hire contract
3 money paid for a trip on public transport
4 where you sit before your flight is announced
5 where you go to get on your plane.

3 Look at the words in blue. Which one:
1 is a verb
2 can be used as an adjective
3 is a noun that means the time spent moving from A to B
4 is a noun that means the same as **3** but can also include the time spent at the destination?

Although you can drive a car at 16 in the US, many car rental companies require you to be at least 25.
Business Travel

Business traveller:
Aileen Cusick

Home town:
Trenton, New Jersey US

Age:
46

Job: Management Consultant

Favourite business destination: Japan, I love travelling on the Shinkansen, those high-speed bullet trains – in the US we're just getting them; in Japan they've had them since 1964.

Frequency: Over 50 trips a year to the Far East.

Tips: Shop around for your hire car as you can get some really good deals, with unlimited mileage and stuff. Always take something to read on the journey and don't forget to buy something on your trip to **take** back to the children.

Best experience. My best experience was actually when I **missed** my connection and I had to **catch** a late night flight which was half empty, so I was upgraded to first class. I met a really interesting guy in the executive departure lounge and two months later we were in business!

Business traveller:
Jacques Caron

Home town:
Lyon, France

Age:
32

Job: Sales Manager

Favourite airport: Hong Kong

Frequency: 20–30 trips a year to European trade shows.

Always takes: to avoid **losing** my luggage I only ever **take** hand-luggage. This also means I don't have to **waste** time waiting ages in the baggage reclaim or break my back by **carrying** kilos of unnecessary weight.

Tips: Always check out flight options yourself before asking your **travel** office to book the trip. Always ask for an upgrade at the gate just before boarding. And remember, taxi fares vary wildly – the most expensive cities are: Los Angeles, Tokyo, Zurich, London, and Amsterdam.

4 Look at the words in **violet**. Which one means:
1 the opposite of 'bring'
2 to transport by hand
3 to get (sometimes only just in time)?

5 Underline the correct words.
1 Waiter. Could you *bring / carry / take* me the menu?
2 We *carried / caught / took* a taxi to the hotel.
3 My bags are so heavy. Could you *bring / carry / catch* them for me, please?
4 Could you *bring / carry / take* this letter to Ms Higa please.
5 I just managed to *bring / catch / take* the bus – it was already moving off!

6 Circle the word or expression in the list on the right that cannot be used with each verb, as in the example.

1 bring   here, (advantage) forward, to someone's attention
2 take   there, time, control, a taxi, a break, care of, up-to-date
3 carry   a load, a suitcase, a shopping bag, out a plan, a flight
4 catch   a bus, a cold, someone's attention, a holiday

Which other verb of the four can the 'odd one out' be used with?

e.g. *advantage – to take advantage*

7 Look at the words in green.
1 Which is used in connection with:
   a objects   **b** transport   **c** activities with no positive result?

2 Which of the words below can *lose*, *miss*, and *waste* be used with? Complete the table. The words in column three can be used with more than one verb.

_____¹ appointments	_____⁴ interest	_____⁷ energy
_____² customers	_____⁵ targets	_____⁸ money
_____³ deadlines	_____⁶ value	_____⁹ opportunities

8 Now read this text taken from a recent book about business travel. In what ways are Aileen Cusick and Jacques Caron typical modern business travellers?

ON THE ROAD IN THE AGE OF THE INTERNET

Despite email and the Internet, businesspeople actually spend more time than ever going to and from meetings. In Silicon Valley, where the technological revolution was born, it is estimated that $3.5 billion is wasted annually because of blocked highways caused by people who still feel the need to get into their cars and travel. One internationally renowned e-guru calculates that he spends 75% of his time 'on the road'. The number of men and women criss-crossing time zones is estimated at 20 million worldwide and this number is likely to double by 2010.

What does the average business traveller look like and how often does he or she pack a suitcase? Research shows that:

● The typical US business traveller spent at least one night away from their home on their most recent business trip (84%), with nearly three quarters staying at a hotel or motel.

● Almost half of US business travellers said that a meeting, trade show or convention was the reason for their latest trip. Frequent business travellers are much more likely to have made their last trip for consulting, sales, or company operations.

● Those who travel for business are more likely to work in the health, legal, and educational services than in the past. The largest proportion of business travellers work in professional and managerial roles.

● The average EU business traveller is a 42-year-old college graduate, a married father who is a professional or manager, with an annual income of at least $75,000.

● In the USA business travellers represent 62% of airline revenues, but they are a much smaller percentage of travellers than leisure travellers. Travelling now represents the third largest expense in most corporations after payroll and information systems; in fact corporations spend more than $175 billion for travel annually. This now involves about 44 million employees and 243 million business trips per year.

9 Complete the sentences with words from the exercises in this section in their correct form. Then ask and answer the questions with a partner.

1 What is the safest way to _____ valuables when you are travelling?
2 Have you ever _____ your passport, suitcases, or ticket?
3 For a _____ of 200–300 km do you prefer to _____ by train or by car?
4 Which is worse: _____ a flight connection or train connection?
5 What things do you always _____ with you when you go on a business _____?
6 How could you avoid _____ time at airports and stations?

GRAMMAR AT WORK

Past continuous and past perfect

1 Which of the following travel problems have you experienced? Which do you think would be the worst?

	you	your partner	speaker 1	speaker 2
long flight delays				
falling ill				
losing baggage				
money problems				
losing valuable items				
hotel problems				
having to ask for help				

(((7.1))) **2** Listen to two people describing their worst business trips.

1 Tick (✓) the problems they mention from the table above.
2 Which experience do you think was the worst.

3 *When I got to the hotel I realized that I hadn't brought enough cash.*
I discovered my bags had never left Paris.

1 Which action happened first – the blue or the pink?
2 Which verb is in the past perfect?

While I was discussing the problem, the fire alarm went off.
They cancelled my flight because they were having problems with the fog.

3 Which action took place in the middle of a longer action – the blue or the pink?
4 Which verb is in the past continuous?

▶ **For more on past tenses, see the Reference section page 126.**

4 Rewrite the questions putting the verbs into the correct form – simple past, past continuous, or past perfect. Then ask and answer the questions with a partner.

1 Where (*be*) the last place you (*visit*) on business? While you (*work*) there you (*have*) any time to do any sightseeing? If so, which sites you (*see*)?
2 Where you last (*go*) on holiday? You (*be*) there before? Before you (*go*), you already (*read*) about the places you (*want*) to visit?
3 While you (*travel*) to work this morning, you (*think*) about work or something else?
4 What you (*do*) this time last week? And an hour ago?
5 When you (*work*) yesterday, you (*have*) time to chat to colleagues?

5 Tell your partner about your worst travel experience. When you are listening to your partner make comments where appropriate, such as *How awful! Oh no! That's terrible! What a nightmare!*

On an average day in the US, Americans see at least three UFOs that are convincing enough to report to the authorities
In One Day

THE INTERVIEW

easyJet

Name: Samantha Day
Position: Marketing Communications Executive
Company: easyJet (founded by Stelios Haji-Ionnou)
Field of Business: Budget air travel
Head Office: Luton, UK

❶ Have you ever travelled on a low-cost airline (e.g. Ryanair, Go, Buzz, easyJet)? What are the advantages and disadvantages of this kind of budget travel.

❷ If you were running a low-cost airline which of the strategies below would you adopt to reduce costs? Which strategies wouldn't you choose? Discuss with a partner.

- ☐ **1** have a uniform fleet of aircraft (i.e. all the same type of plane)
- ☐ **2** require cabin crew to purchase their own uniforms
- ☐ **3** refund passengers if there are delays
- ☐ **4** have a flat management structure (i.e. few levels of hierarchy)
- ☐ **5** be a ticketless airline (i.e. direct sales over the Internet)
- ☐ **6** base aircraft in secondary rather than major airports
- ☐ **7** only fly on very popular routes
- ☐ **8** pay pilots by the kilometre
- ☐ **9** eliminate in-flight magazines and meals

e.g. *I would try to have all the same type of plane because that would make maintenance costs, getting spare parts, etc. much easier. I don't know if I would make staff buy their own uniforms because …*

(((7.2))) ❸ Listen to Samantha Day talking about reasons for the company's success. Tick (✓) the strategies from ❷ that she mentions.

4 Listen again. Besides cost reductions, what are the other benefits to easyJet of strategies 1–5? Complete the sentences below.

1 Having a uniform fleet means …
2 The fact that cabin crew purchase their own uniforms means …
3 The consequence of refunding passengers when there are delays is …
4 The advantage of the flat management structure is …
5 Selling tickets on the Internet makes it possible to …

Listening tip

5 Just as we need punctuation to help us read, speech is also punctuated. We punctuate our speech using pauses and by stressing key words.

Underline what you think the key words are in this passage from the interview.

cabin crew / for example / as well / have to purchase their own uniforms / which means that / they take care of their clothing / a lot more than they would / if we provided them for free / we also motivate ourselves / by having quite a strong refund policy / which essentially means that / if a passenger's delayed / for more than an hour / they're entitled to a refund / or a free transfer / to a different flight.

(((7.3))) **6** Listen and check your answers.

1 What do you notice about how the key words are pronounced?
2 Are the other words said more quickly or more slowly than the key words?
3 If you only understand the key words, can you still understand the general meaning?

(((7.4))) **7** Now practise listening for key words. Listen to Samantha answering the question 'How important is new technology in your business?' and fill in the gaps with one or more words.

Well, it's essential to us _____ .[1] It's, it's the only _____[2] in which we can _____[3] without incurring a great deal of _____[4] and having to change our whole _____[5] plan. The _____[6] has obviously been a _____[7] factor in our _____[8] because we have a _____[9] office here at _____ .[10] Then everything we have is _____ ,[11] which means everybody's got an _____[12] desktop. So you have your own in _____[13] on your _____[14] and your own outbasket on your _____ ,[15] so no _____[16] is _____ .[17] Because we are a ticketless _____ ,[18] which is one thing that I forgot to mention in the way we keep our costs down, then we've got an _____ ,[19] reservation system which gives _____[20] a confirmation _____[21] and that's all that they need to _____ .[22]

Talking point

8 What new technologies has your company adopted recently? How effective are they? Do you think it is important to use state-of-the-art equipment and methods?

Four out of ten UK employers believe the time it takes to get to work causes serious recruitment difficulties. In reaction 10% of organizations offer the option of working from home, 14% offer subsidized parking, 7% travel subsidies, 2% transport schemes, and 1% car pools.
Sunday Telegraph

BUSINESS SKILLS

Recommending and suggesting

1 If you could travel instantly to any place in the world for one day, where would you choose and why?

(((7.5))) **2** Listen to a Moroccan businessman talking about places to visit in Casablanca and Marrakech.

1 What building does he recommend visiting in Casablanca?
2 Apart from the main square, what one other thing does he recommend in Marrakech?
3 Is he more enthusiastic about Casablanca or Marrakech?

3 Listen again. Are the following true (T) or false (F)?

1 The Hassan II Mosque is next to the sea.
2 Marrakech is a three-day drive from Casablanca.
3 He recommends setting off late at night.
4 The market is interesting but there are unpleasant smells.
5 The market mainly sells food.

(((7.6))) **4** Try to fill in the gaps from these extracts from the conversation from memory. Then listen and check your answers.

Asking for suggestions

☐ _____ to Casablanca, is that an interesting place to visit?

☐ And would you _____ going to Marrakech?

☐ I've heard there's a big market? Is it _____ going there?

Giving recommendations

☐ Yes I would definitely recommend _____ to Marrakech.

☐ I _____ doing it early in the morning.

☐ I would definitely explore it if _____ you.

☐ You _____ also visit the mosque.

5 Work with a partner. Talk about a place you know well and you think he / she might like to visit. Make recommendations about the following:

travel to the place	restaurants	hotels	museums
travel in the place	local dishes	sightseeing	bars / cafés
shopping	places to avoid	night life	people

6 What steps would you recommend to help prevent the situations below happening when you travel? Exchange ideas with a partner:

getting lost	being overcharged for things
losing your passport	being robbed
missing your flight	having communication problems

e.g. *To prevent getting lost you could try and buy a map of the city before you go.*

7 Look at the travel situations *a–e* below. Write two questions: **1** that you would ask and, **2** that the staff / personnel would ask you in each situation.

e.g. **a** *Can I check in here? Do you have any hand luggage?*

a checking in your luggage at the airport

b finding your luggage at the baggage reclaim

c buying a train ticket

d paying for your hotel room

e renting a car

(((7.7))) **8** Listen to the following dialogues 1–5 and match them with the situations *a–e* in **7**.

1 _____ **2** _____ **3** _____ **4** _____ **5** _____

Check your answers, and your answers to **7**, with the tapescript on page 147.

9 Now you are going to practise some other travel situations. Student A, turn to File 5 on page 109. Student B, look at File 16 on page 114.

AOL once stated that of the estimated 30 million email messages each day, about 30% on average were unsolicited commercial email. Many companies such as AOL and Hotmail employ full-time staff specifically to deal with junk-mail-related problems and the receivers pay the costs.

Guardian

EMAIL

Requests and replies

 Look at the cyber tip points below. Which ones refer to:

a replying to emails   **b** making requests   **c** both?

CYBERTIP

Requests and replies

- ✦ Any correspondence with other businesses presents an image of you and your company, so make sure that your message is accurate, professional, and your meaning is obvious. Don't write to impress; write to explain.

- ✦ If appropriate, identify yourself, then detail the information that your reader needs to understand your purpose for writing.

- ✦ Make sure it is clear which part of an email you are referring to – always provide the context.

- ✦ If you're quoting somebody's message it is sometimes helpful to quote the relevant parts, instead of sending the whole thing back.

- ✦ When you receive inquiries make sure you answer all the queries, not just some of them.

- ✦ Be careful with use of pronouns e.g. *them, it* (make sure it will be clear to the reader what these pronouns refer to).

- ✦ Organize any questions you have in the most appropriate order.

- ✦ End with an action point: suggest what reader's next move should be or your own. Give the exact information the reader will need to get back to you (*who, when, where, how*).

- ✦ Thank the reader.

2 You have received this email on your return from a trip abroad to install a software package for a client. Write replies that you could insert into the text after each paragraph. Use the information in brackets to help you.

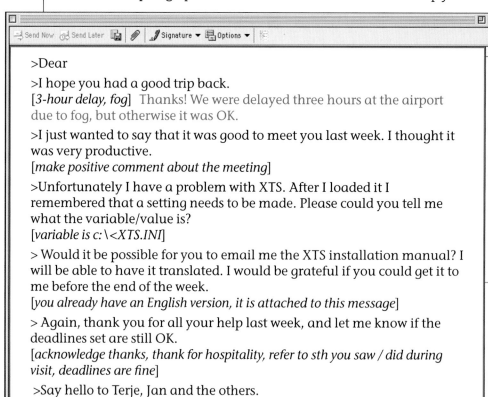

>Dear

>I hope you had a good trip back.
[*3-hour delay, fog*]   Thanks! We were delayed three hours at the airport due to fog, but otherwise it was OK.

>I just wanted to say that it was good to meet you last week. I thought it was very productive.
[*make positive comment about the meeting*]

>Unfortunately I have a problem with XTS. After I loaded it I remembered that a setting needs to be made. Please could you tell me what the variable/value is?
[*variable is c:\<XTS.INI*]

> Would it be possible for you to email me the XTS installation manual? I will be able to have it translated. I would be grateful if you could get it to me before the end of the week.
[*you already have an English version, it is attached to this message*]

> Again, thank you for all your help last week, and let me know if the deadlines set are still OK.
[*acknowledge thanks, thank for hospitality, refer to sth you saw / did during visit, deadlines are fine*]

>Say hello to Terje, Jan and the others.
[*make suitable comment and close*]

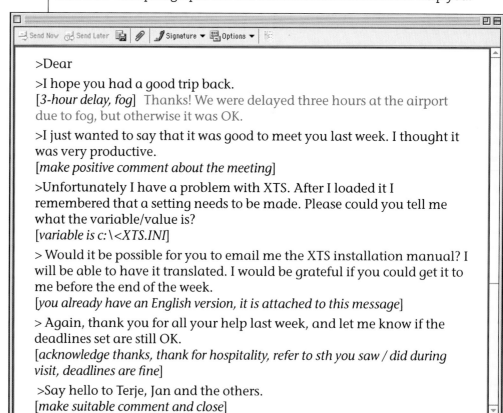

3 You have received the email below from a contact you met at a conference in Geneva last month. Underline the parts in the email that you need to respond to. Then write a reply, using the information below to help you.

> *You are late in replying to José's email (invent excuse). You remember meeting José. You are still interested in the Spanish market. You want to meet but you are unavailable next month. You could possibly go to Spain instead. You need to see a proposal in writing to show to your colleagues first before you make any decisions. You attach a copy of the paper.*

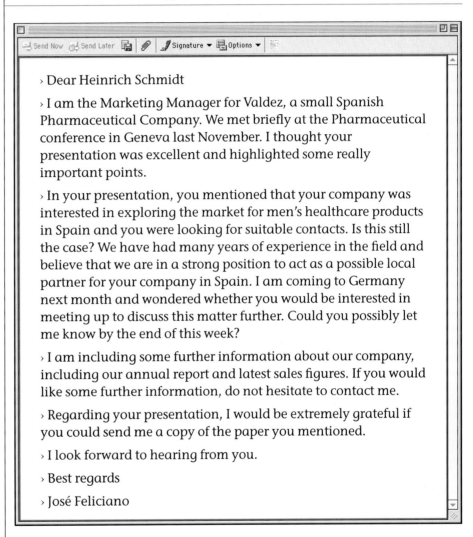

> Dear Heinrich Schmidt

> I am the Marketing Manager for Valdez, a small Spanish Pharmaceutical Company. We met briefly at the Pharmaceutical conference in Geneva last November. I thought your presentation was excellent and highlighted some really important points.

> In your presentation, you mentioned that your company was interested in exploring the market for men's healthcare products in Spain and you were looking for suitable contacts. Is this still the case? We have had many years of experience in the field and believe that we are in a strong position to act as a possible local partner for your company in Spain. I am coming to Germany next month and wondered whether you would be interested in meeting up to discuss this matter further. Could you possibly let me know by the end of this week?

> I am including some further information about our company, including our annual report and latest sales figures. If you would like some further information, do not hesitate to contact me.

> Regarding your presentation, I would be extremely grateful if you could send me a copy of the paper you mentioned.

> I look forward to hearing from you.

> Best regards

> José Feliciano

4 Read the emails in **2** and **3** again. Underline all the different ways of making requests.

5 Read the tips above and write request emails based on the notes below.

1 Arrange a demonstration of a supplier's product at your company's headquarters. Ask if this is possible, and then for a convenient date and time.

2 You are interested in this same supplier's products for your own private use. Ask for prices, parts lists, details of available technical information, and maintenance manuals. All are needed asap.

3 An invoice is nine months overdue. You've chased the client several times and now want immediate settlement. No new orders can be processed until the client settles the overdue balance on his / her account.

NUL112297 Campbell's Soup Cans, 1965 (silkscreen on canvas) by Andy Warhol (1930-87). Private Collection/Bridgeman Art Library. ©The Andy Warhol Foundation for the Visual Arts, Inc./DACS, London, 2002. Trademarks Licensed by Campbell Soup Company. All Rights Reserved.

8 PRODUCTS

KICK OFF

Discuss with a partner – In which year do you think these products were put on the market? Compare with the key on page 106.

photocopier	Ford Model T	video recorder	paper clip
paperback book	fridge	Boeing 707	radio

THE INTERVIEW

Muji

Name: Kathryn Dighton
Position: Press Relations Consultant
Company: Muji
Field of Business: Retailing
Head Office: Tokyo, Japan

❶ Read the text below about the concept behind Muji, the Japanese retail company. Fill in the gaps, using the words and expressions from in the box.

label	simple	plain	basic
functional	brand	who	what

Muji has an extremely strong concept behind it. Literally translated, *Mujirushiryohin*, which is the company's original name, means 'no-_____¹ or no-_____² quality goods.' The idea is that the value of the product lies in _____³ it is, not in _____⁴ it is designed by. So, we don't visibly brand the goods. The key criteria of the concept are that Muji goods should be very, very_____⁵; they should therefore be _____⁶ in design, but never bland, and _____⁷ rather than decorative for decoration's sake. Also the goods should be realized in _____⁸, understated colours and the range should be a fully comprehensive lifestyle range.

concept (*n*) – an idea or principle
range (*n*) – a set of products of a particular type
brand (*v*) – put a label on
bland (*adj*) – with no strong colour or taste, uninteresting
key (*adj*) **criteria** (*n*) – most important principles

(((8.1))) **2** Listen and check your answers. Does the Muji concept appeal to you?

(((8.2))) **3** Now listen to Kathryn talking about how the company has developed. Are the following true (T) or false (F)?

1 The company was set up with a wide range of products on offer.
2 The same items have been bestsellers for a long time.
3 Muji products are trialled in Japan before being launched in the UK.
4 There are as many Muji outlets in the UK as there are in Japan.
5 Many Muji shops operate independently on a franchise basis.
6 Stores only sell a limited range of items.

4 Listen again and choose the correct answer.

1 The company was originally set up in:
   a 1918   **b** 1980   **c** 1991
2 Muji first came to the UK in:
   a 1980   **b** 1981   **c** 1991
3 The futon bed sells for:
   a £265   **b** £275   **c** £285
4 Muji baby wear will be launched on:
   a 4 Sept   **b** 13 Sept   **c** 14 Sept
5 In Japan the number of outlets is currently:
   a 214   **b** 215   **c** 240   **d** 250
6 In the UK the number of outlets is currently:
   a 13   **b** 14   **c** 30   **d** 40
7 In numbers of square feet, a typical Muji store is:
   a 3000   **b** 4000   **c** 30000   **d** 40000

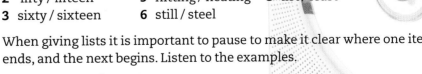

Listening tip

(((8.3))) **5** Listen to the pronunciation of *thirty* and *thirteen*, and *still* and *steel*. What is the main difference? Practise saying the sentences.

1 I think initially there were *thirty* items in the range.
2 We're currently trading here with *thirteen* stores.
3 There are certain items which *still* hit our bestseller list each week.
4 We have a very flexible range of perforated *steel* furniture.

(((8.4))) **6** Listen and underline the word you hear.

1 thirty / thirteen   4 forty / fourteen   7 living / leaving
2 fifty / fifteen   5 hitting / heating   8 list / least
3 sixty / sixteen   6 still / steel

(((8.5))) **7** When giving lists it is important to pause to make it clear where one item ends, and the next begins. Listen to the examples.

1 **a** 50, 9, 8   **b** 59, 8
2 **a** furniture, catalogues, and samples   **b** furniture catalogues, and samples

Now listen to ten lists and decide whether you hear two items or three.

8 ## Talking point

Muji is innovative in that it creates high-quality products from recycled materials. Can you think of any other innovative companies? Is your company innovative? In what ways?

GRAMMAR AT WORK

The passive

1 Look at these pairs of sentences.

a
1 *Muji* **was set up** *in 1980.*
2 *New products* **are trialled** *in Japan.*

b
1 *A businessman* **set up** *Muji in 1980.*
2 *Muji* **trials** *all new products in Japan.*

1 Which sentences are active and which are passive?
2 What information do the **b** sentences contain which is missing from the **a** sentences?
3 Complete the rules in the box below.

The passive is formed with the verb _____ in the appropriate tense and the past participle of the main verb:

present: *is / are* + past participle

future: _____ *be* + past participle

conditional: _____ *be* + past participle

past: _____ / _____ + past participle

present perfect: *has / have been* + past participle

▶ For more on the passive, see the Reference section page 125.

2 Underline the correct active or passive form of the questions in the quiz. Then work with a partner to try to guess the answers.

QUIZ: BUSINESS TRIVIA

1 How much time *spends / is spent* by human resource managers on reading a resumé?
  a 30 seconds to 4 minutes
  b 5–15 minutes
  c quarter of an hour to half an hour

2 What percentage of the world's goods *produced / were produced* in Britain in 1870?
  a 13%
  b 20%
  c 30%
  d 36%
  e 40%

3 What percentage of the new products that *will make / will be made* next year are unlikely to become a commercial success?
  a 8%
  b 18%
  c 50%
  d 80%

4 What percentage of staff *would not recommend / would not be recommended* their own organization's products and services?
  a 13%
  b 14%
  c 30%
  d 40%

5 What are the chances of being in the bathroom when you *want / are wanted* by the boss?
  a 1 in 4
  b 1 in 13
  c 1 in 30
  d 1 in 40

6 How many employees in the UK *have bought / have been bought* gifts for their bosses?
  a 1 in 3
  b 1 in 10
  c 1 in 30
  d 1 in 50

7 What ratio of Americans a year *injure / are injured* severely enough by 'desk accessories' (even pens and pencils) to need emergency room treatment in hospital?
  a 1 in 5,000
  b 1 in 50,000
  c 1 in 500,000
  d 1 in 5,000,000

8 What percentage of office workers *daydream / are daydreamt* about being CEO of their company?
  a 59%
  b 63%
  c 67%
  d 73%
  e 77%

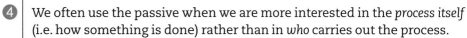

(((8.6))) **3** You are going to hear an extract from a business chat show on the radio. Listen and check your answers to **2**. Then compare with the key on page 106.

4 We often use the passive when we are more interested in the *process itself* (i.e. how something is done) rather than in *who* carries out the process.

Write a brief description of what happens at each stage in the process of buying something online. Use the diagram and prompts below to help you, as in the example. (Note that only some of the sentences will be in the passive.)

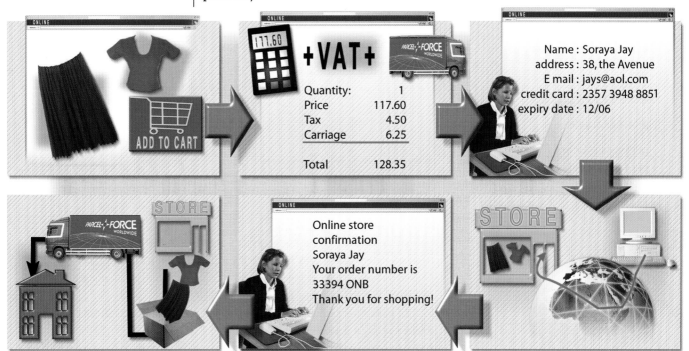

1 First / find items / want to buy / and put / electronic shopping cart.
First find the items you want to buy and put them in the electronic shopping cart.

2 When / finish shopping / your purchases / add up. Tax and carriage costs / then include.
When you have finished shopping your purchases are added up. Tax and ...

3 Then fill out / online order form / carriage information.

4 In order to pay, type in / credit card number, plus other information / that require / merchant.

5 Next, credit card information / encrypt / and send / merchant.

6 At this point, receive / on-screen confirmation.

7 Finally, your goods / collect from warehouse / then package / and send to you.

5 What typical processes – e.g. delivery of products, invoice processing, dealing with enquiries – does your job / the work of your company involve?

1 Make notes to help you to describe one of these processes. Use the expressions below to help you organize and sequence your ideas.

first(ly)	next	when you've done that	when this has been done
second(ly)	then	at this stage / point	finally

2 Work in pairs and take it in turns to describe your processes.

WORDS AT WORK

Marketing

1 Look at the table below. Apart from cost, which factor plays the major role in how you decide to purchase the products and services? Put a cross in the corresponding column.

	advertising, direct marketing (e.g. mailings)	appearance, design, wrapping, packaging	expert opinion (on TV, in specialized journals)	recommendation from friends and relatives
computers / organizers				
flights / hotels / car rentals				
cars				
movies / books / CDs				
Internet provider				
games (e.g. board, games, computer games)				

2 Check your answers to **1** by reading the facts below.

- 65% of customers who bought a Palm organizer, a leader in hand-held devices, told the makers that they had heard about it from another person.
- 43% of people use their family as a source of information on places to visit or flights, hotels, or rental cars.
- 57% of customers in one car dealership in California learnt about the dealership by word of mouth.
- 53% of moviegoers rely to some extent on a recommendation from someone they know, according to market analysis and research.
- 100%, almost, of Hotmail's first 12 million subscribers (only 18 months after its launch) learnt about the provider from friends emailing them, with the line at the bottom of the message saying 'Get your free email at Hotmail.com' – one of the simplest yet most effective marketing campaigns ever.
- 100%, almost, of the 20 million copies of the board game Trivial Pursuit were sold with no advertising in 1984. The marketing department sent copies to celebrities mentioned in the questions. Hollywood parties were organized, copies were given away on radio quiz shows, and buyers before the launch of the product at the New York Toy Fair in 1983 were mailed random cards to stimulate their interest.

3 The statistics in **2** come from a book by Seth Godin who analysed the way people buy products and services simply through word of mouth, or 'buzz'. Godin is also the inventor of 'permission marketing'. Read the text opposite to find out what this type of marketing is.

PERMISSION MARKETING

The most common form of marketing is advertising, which, Seth Godin, an American marketing guru, calls 'interruption marketing'. Advertising is annoying, expensive, and amazingly ineffective. Today's consumers are so saturated with information that ads often fail to leave a mark, even if seen or heard over and over again. Additionally, most ads are simply irrelevant to the majority of people who see them.

Effective marketing, again according to Godin, is about developing a long-term relationship with your customers, and, as with all types of relationships, it requires a tremendous amount of work. Given this effort, however, the Internet offers great opportunity as a medium for direct marketing. Godin has become famous for his work on identifying the unique ways in which the Internet can be used as a marketing tool. One of these ways is permission marketing. The concept is simple. You get permission to market to a customer usually by offering some incentive – for example, a special discount or a gift. Once you obtain this initial permission, you try to obtain higher levels of permission (to market other products) by offering other rewards. Customers may opt out at any time, and once they do, you must stop marketing to them.

A highly successful example of permission marketing is frequent flyer programmes. When you join one of these programmes, you give airlines permission to track where and how frequently you travel in exchange for points that lead to free tickets. With this information, airlines can effectively market other services to you, services in which you're likely to be interested. For example, if you make frequent trips to Hong Kong, the airline might send you special offers for hotels and transport in Hong Kong.

---

interruption (n) – sth that – for a short time – stops an activity or a situation
saturated (adj) – completely filled with sth
irrelevant (adj) – not important to the situation
incentive (n) – sth that makes you want to do sth
discount (n) – reduction, money that is taken off the usual cost of sth
opt out (v) – to choose not to take part in sth

4 Read the text again and answer the following questions.

1 Why do you think Godin uses the expression 'interruption marketing' to describe traditional television advertising?
2 Why has this type of marketing become ineffective?

5 What is the difference in meaning between *market* and *marketing*? Which word describes an activity, and which can describe a place or concept? Complete the diagrams below with the words in the box.

analysis	budget	campaign	leader
share	department	strategy	led

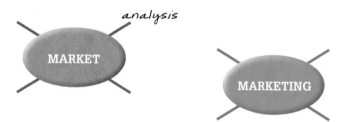

6 Complete the sentences below with *market, marketing,* or *product(s)* and one of the words in italics. Then ask and answer the questions with a partner.

1 How big is your company's _____ *share / value / forces?*
2 Does your company consider itself a _____ *leader / analyst / research?*
3 How much time is spent on _____ *line / development / life cycle?*
4 What is the most appropriate _____ *research / mix / strategy* for your company – direct mailings, free samples, word of mouth, other (what)?
5 What is the average *image / launch / life cycle* of your _____ ?

BUSINESS SKILLS

Generating and reacting to ideas

1 Discuss these questions.

1 Is having new ideas important in your job? Do you think you are good at generating new ideas?

2 Which do you prefer:
   a to have your own ideas about things
   b to generate ideas in a group with other people (brainstorm)?

3 Look at the tips for brainstorming below, and fill in the gaps using the words in the box.

judgements	participates	fun	time limit
perspectives	consideration	chairperson	

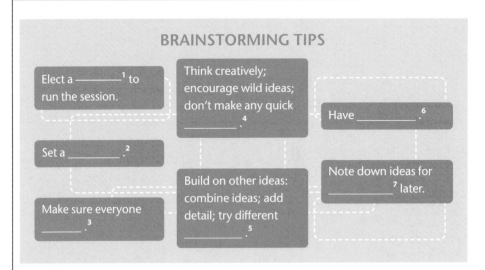

BRAINSTORMING TIPS

Elect a ———¹ to run the session.

Think creatively; encourage wild ideas; don't make any quick _____ ⁴

Have _____ ⁶ .

Set a _____ ²

Build on other ideas: combine ideas; add detail; try different _____ ⁵

Note down ideas for _____ ⁷ later.

Make sure everyone _____ ³

4 Are there any of the tips you don't agree with? Are there any that you will try to use in the future?

(((8.7))) **2** You are going to hear an extract from a brainstorming meeting. The purpose is to find ways to promote a children's game which involves collecting cards of TV cartoon characters. Listen and answer the questions.

1 What marketing idea does Sanjay, the first speaker, suggest?
2 Why don't the other speakers like it?
3 What idea do they come up with as an alternative?

3 Listen again. Number these expressions in the order you hear them, as in the example.

___ Could I just finish what I was saying?

___ Exactly!

___ It might be a good idea to …

___ I'm not sure I agree with you.

___ Do you see what we're getting at?

___ Sorry to interrupt but …

1 What's your view on this?

4 Now match the expressions with the functions below.

a react positively to an idea
b show reservations
c interrupt
d get people involved

e check understanding
f make a suggestion
g manage an interruption

Think of one other different expression for each function. Compare ideas with a partner.

5 Apart from by word of mouth from friends, how do you hear about new films? What were the last few films that you went to see? What influenced you to choose these films?

6 Work in small groups. You are part of a marketing team. You are going to have a meeting to brainstorm ideas to promote the following four films:

– an adventure cartoon for children
– a romantic / love comedy
– a science-fiction film
– a mystery / horror film

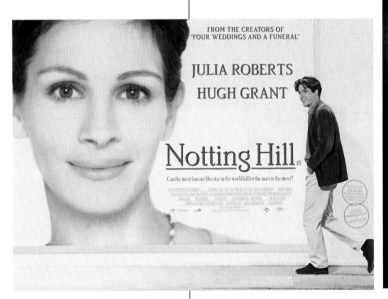

1 Elect a chairperson whose job it is to manage the meeting and decide on the four films you are going to talk about. Spend a maximum of two minutes brainstorming marketing ideas for each film. (You can use the two films illustrated in the posters or you can think of new ones.)
2 Look at the key on page 107 which gives you information about ways in which various Hollywood films have been marketed.
   Discuss which strategies you would use for each of your four films. Answer the questions for each strategy to help you decide how you would apply it for each film.
3 Choose one of your films and plan a marketing campaign based on the strategies on page 107, but including any other ideas of your own.
4 Each group presents their campaign to the class. The class decides which is the most interesting and original campaign.

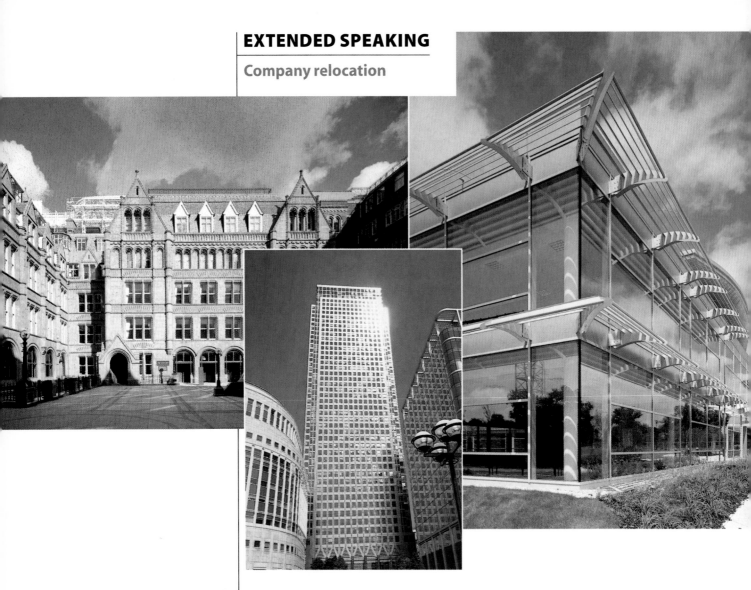

1 Discuss these questions.

1 How long has your company been in its current location? What are the advantages and disadvantages of the location?

2 Has the company changed its premises in recent years, or do you think it is likely to in the future? Why?

3 What are the problems involved in relocation?

2 Your company is expanding rapidly. To deal with the increased business and the increasing number of personnel you need more office / factory / warehouse space.

The management have identified three possible strategies.

STRATEGY 1
Make better use of space already available and / or extend the existing premises.

STRATEGY 2
Find additional premises (possibly more than one, if departments can be divided up).

STRATEGY 3
Move the whole operation to completely new premises.

3 Work in three groups. Each group has to investigate one of the options above. Consider the following:

- logistical feasibility
- likely cost
- impact on neighbouring environment
- impact on ongoing work within the company
- effect on the company's image
- how popular the change will be among the workforce.
- impact on communication (both internal, and external with customers)
- the feasibility of restructuring and how it could be made
- impact in terms of transport, accommodation, schools for staff with children.

1 In your group, discuss all the possible problems connected with your strategy.
2 Draw up a list of advantages and disadvantages, and brainstorm ideas for solutions to the problems.
3 Prepare to present your solution to the other groups. Decide who will say what. Prepare some visual aids to make your presentation as interesting and persuasive as possible.
4 The groups take it in turns to present their strategy to the other two groups.
5 When all three groups have presented their strategies, vote to decide which is the best.

Current location

Expand existing premises
cost: 16 million euros building
time: 2 years

Alternative location
cost: 7 million euros
city centre: 80 km (no public transport)

9 TRANSACTIONS

KICK OFF

1 Look at the picture. How have financial transactions changed over the years?

2 Which of the following banking services have you used? Tick the relevant boxes and then compare with a partner.

- ☐ current account (cheque book, monthly statements, usually no interest)
- ☐ savings account (high interest rate, notice for withdrawals)
- ☐ overdraft (when you owe the bank money on your account)
- ☐ standing orders and direct debits (to pay regular bills)
- ☐ credit transfers (to send money from one account to another)
- ☐ mortgage (for buying a house) or loans (for buying other things)

3 Which is the most important factor for you when choosing a bank?

- ☐ services that are easily accessible
- ☐ competitive rates of interest
- ☐ helpful and understanding staff
- ☐ fast transactions

THE INTERVIEW

The Co-operative Bank

Name: David Smith
Position: Group PR Manager
Company: Co-operative Bank
Field of Business: Banking
Head Office: Manchester, UK

In 1992 the Co-operative Bank was the first bank in the UK to publish an ethical stance includes a statement on which industries it will and will not do business with.

1 | Read the key dates in the history of the Co-operative Bank. Does your bank offer any of the same services?

1973 First bank to announce free banking for all personal current account customers in credit.	**1992** Official launch of first telephone banking service.
1982 First high-interest cheque account for personal customers.	**1997** World's first biodegradable Visa credit card.
1991 First bank to offer a guaranteed 'Free for Life' Visa Gold Card.	**1999** Launched Smile, the Internet bank.

(((9.1))) **2** | Listen to this interview with the PR Manager of the Co-operative Bank and answer the questions.

 1 How do customers benefit from the bank's ethical stance?
 2 How does the bank decide who it will and will not do business with?
 3 Who does the Co-operative Bank not do business with?
 4 What impact does this have on the bank's competitiveness?
 5 What percentage of profit is associated with the ethical stance?
 6 Which of the 'firsts' in **1** above does David mention?

(((9.2))) **3** | Listen to these other questions from the interview and fill in the gaps.

 1 What _____ if the Third World debt _____ ?
 2 What _____ if the Third World debt _____ ?
 3 If _____ just one currency in the world _____ a good thing?
 4 Some traders in commercial banks in London get annual bonuses of over a million pounds. If you _____ such a bonus what _____ it on?
 5 If you _____ in the banking field what _____ to do?
 6 What _____ if technology shares _____ again?

(((9.3))) **4** | Now you will hear David answering four of the questions in **3**. Match each answer *a–d* with the appropriate question.

 a ____   **b** ____   **c** ____   **d** ____

Listening tip

(((9.4))) **5** | How is the *w* pronounced in the following words: /w/, /h/, or silent (not pronounced)?

1 would	**4** what	**7** who	**10** answer	**13** know
2 wood	**5** which	**8** whole	**11** overdrawn	**14** borrow
3 will	**6** white	**9** why	**12** forward	**15** new

Now listen and check your answers.

(((9.5))) **6** | Listen and underline the word you hear. Then practise reading aloud.

1 is / his	**4** art / heart	**7** angry / hungry	**10** dole / doll
2 it / hit	**5** eye / high	**8** won't / want	
3 own / one	**6** note / not	**9** road / rod	

7 | ## Talking point

What would you do with a million-dollar bonus?

WORDS AT WORK

Understanding headlines

Japan announces huge trade surplus

Oil prices up 10%

Housing boom hits peak

Techno shares crash

Top fast food chain assets frozen

Exchange rates axed: whole world to adopt dollar in 2020

20% inflation next year?

Worried US cuts interest rate again

Third world debt cancelled

Giant pay-offs for departing CEOs

1 Discuss these questions with a partner.

1 How often do you read the financial news? Is it easy to understand?
2 How do you prefer to read financial news – online or in a newspaper?

2 Look at the headlines above. What do you notice about the grammar and vocabulary? Find one or more examples of headlines that:

a don't contain a verb
b contain strings of two or more nouns
c use the present simple to refer to a past event
d use an infinitive to refer to the future
e omit articles (*a* and *the*) and / or auxilary verbs (*be, have*).

3 Look again at the headlines. Find words which mean:

1	an excess quantity	s_____
2	a period of rapid increase in sales	b_____
3	an increase in prices and fall in the value of money	i_____
4	anything of value owned by a company	a_____
5	an amount of money owed	d_____
6	to fall suddenly	c_____
7	the system for how one currency is valued against another	e_____ r_____
8	a charge for the use of borrowed money	i_____
9	the highest point of rise	p_____
10	money paid to end an employment contract early	p_____ o_____

4 Write the opposites of the words in 1–5 in **3**.

1 de_ _ t **2** sl_ _ p **3** de_ _ _ _ _ _ n **4** lia_ _ _ _ _ y **5** cr_ _ _ t

5 Match three of the headlines in **②** with the extracts from the reports below.

1

As executive demands grow, so agreements with employers become extremely complicated. Some exit deals take more than a year to work out. Inevitably, this generates high legal bills. A prominent term in all three agreements made public this week is that the lawyers be paid by the companies involved. No doubt the former executives believe them to be worth every cent.

2

Property prices are set to rise by little more than the rate of inflation, according to figures issued yesterday. The Council for Mortgage Lenders, which issued the data, has also radically revised its prediction for house price growth this year after admitting that the market's strong performance had taken it by surprise.

3

So far this year the federal reserve has slashed three percentage points off borrowing costs, its most aggressive rate-cutting campaign since the last recession. Yesterday's quarter per cent cut brings the cost of borrowing in the US down to 3.5 per cent.

Which words in the reports helped you to match the headlines?

6 Short words are often used in headlines to save space (e.g. *axe* = abolish, *jobless* = unemployed people, *top* = very important). Here are some common ones. Match them with their meanings, as in the example.

1	aid	**a**	agreement, bargain
2	ban	**b**	dismissal from job
3	deal	**c**	help
4	cut	**d**	forbid, prohibit
5	block	**e**	sudden increase, rise suddenly
6	stake	**f**	reduction
7	sack	**g**	holding in a company
8	slump	**h**	sudden reduction or economic depression
9	poll	**i**	stop, delay
10	surge	**j**	election, public opinion survey

7 The words in 1–10 in **⑥** are not only used in headlines. Complete the sentences below with the correct word, then ask and answer the questions with a partner.

1 Does your company have a _____ in other companies? If so, which ones?

2 If you had to conduct an opinion _____ regarding what clients think of your company what questions would you ask?

3 If your boss was given the _____ , would you like to take his / her job?

4 How much financial _____ does your government give to the unemployed? Should it give more or less?

5 If you could make new laws in your country what activities would you like to _____ ?

The highest ever value note issued in the USA was $100,000 for transactions between the Federal Reserve and the Treasury Department. Until 1939, £1000 notes were commonly used in the UK for house purchases.

The Economist

GRAMMAR AT WORK

First and second conditionals

1 Look at these sentences and answer the questions below.

first conditional (*if* + present, + *will* + infinitive)

a *If share prices **go** down again, we'**ll lose** a lot of money.*
b *If I **see** her I'**ll ask** her about the funding.*

second conditional (*if* + simple past, + *would* / *might* /*could* + infinitive)

c *If you **had** a bonus of a million pounds what **would** you **spend** it on?*
d *If we **used** a new logo people **might not recognize** it.*

Which sentence(s):

1 refer to a real or very possible future situation?
2 refer to a hypothetical or less probable future situation?
3 indicate a tentative observation (i.e. the speaker or is not certain about what he / she is saying, or is making a suggestion)?

▶ **For more on conditionals, see the Reference section page 118.**

2 Underline an appropriate form and then complete the sentences. How likely is it that these situations will happen?

1 If I only *work / worked* four days a week, _____
2 _____ if I *don't / didn't* work for this company.
3 _____ if the weather *is / was* nice this weekend.
4 If I *get / got* a pay rise, _____
5 If I *don't / didn't* practise my English, _____

3 Put the sentences below into the second conditional, using the correct form of the verbs in italics. Then ask and answer the questions with your partner.

1 You *make* a serious error at work but no one *can* possibly trace the error to you, you *say* nothing?
2 You *give* a former colleague / friend a reference even if they *be* not good at their job?
3 After months of negotiation, if you *be* about to sign the contract and you *notice* a mistake in a clause which would greatly benefit your company, you *go* ahead and sign the contract?
4 You *stay* with your company if they *move* their premises to another town or country?

4 We often use conditionals to consider possibilities – *what would happen if …* .

1 In your group discuss ideas for updating your company's image. Brainstorm suggestions and then evaluate your ideas, in order to decide the best course of action. Consider the following:
   – what the current image is
   – how the image could / needs to be changed
   – what changing the image would involve
   – what would be gained (and lost) by changing it.

2 Alternatively, if you all work for different companies, discuss ideas for cutting costs in companies in general.
   – what typical costs are (e.g. salaries, travel)
   – which costs could feasibly be cut
   – what savings would be made
   – what consequences cuts might have.

(((9.6))) **5** Conditionals are also frequently used in negotiations. Listen to these three dialogues and match them with the photos *a–c* at the top of page 90.
   1 ____   **2** ____   **3** ____

6 Play this game with a partner. Each situation in the boxes represents a negotiation scenario. Improvise the situations, including as many conditional sentences as you can. (You have a maximum of one minute per negotiation.) You get one point for each conditional you use. The winner is the player with the most points at the end.

   e.g: A: *If I do your homework will you fix my computer?*
        B: *I think the teacher might be angry if you did my homework.*

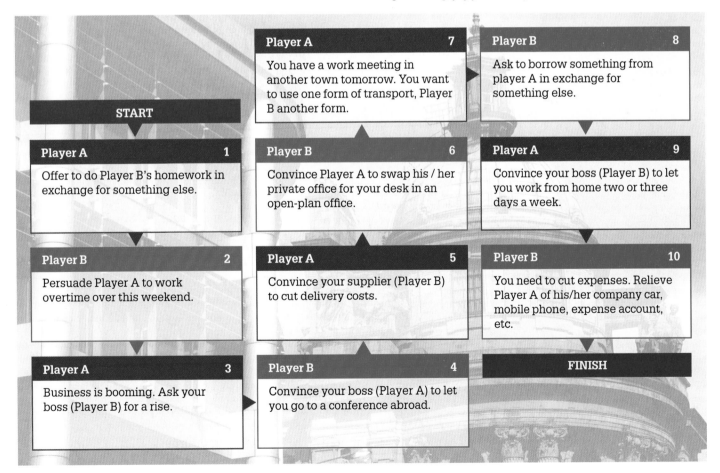

START

Player A 1
Offer to do Player B's homework in exchange for something else.

Player B 2
Persuade Player A to work overtime over this weekend.

Player A 3
Business is booming. Ask your boss (Player B) for a rise.

Player A 7
You have a work meeting in another town tomorrow. You want to use one form of transport, Player B another form.

Player B 6
Convince Player A to swap his / her private office for your desk in an open-plan office.

Player A 5
Convince your supplier (Player B) to cut delivery costs.

Player B 4
Convince your boss (Player A) to let you go to a conference abroad.

Player B 8
Ask to borrow something from player A in exchange for something else.

Player A 9
Convince your boss (Player B) to let you work from home two or three days a week.

Player B 10
You need to cut expenses. Relieve Player A of his/her company car, mobile phone, expense account, etc.

FINISH

BUSINESS SKILLS

Negotiating

 'We negotiate every day of our lives'. Do you agree? Think of ways that you negotiate and bargain in your everyday lives. Work in pairs and add to the lists for the following categories:

1 for yourself at work, e.g. *overtime*
2 for your company at work, e.g. *delivery dates*
3 with shop and service personnel, e.g. *car mechanics*
4 with children, e.g. *food*
5 with friends, e.g. *deciding what to do.*

 Do you have good negotiating skills? Try this test and find out. Choose what you think is the best answer and then discuss with your partner. Finally, compare with the key on page 107.

QUIZ: TEST YOUR NEGOTIATING SKILLS

1 Your negotiating partner is determined to beat you down by 5% on your original offer. Do you:
   a say you can come down by 2% and no more?
   b say you can't move from your original offer?
   c suggest that you have another look at the overall deal?

2 During a meeting with negotiating partners from a different country / culture, you notice that they are very silent and ask few questions; do you assume this means:
   a they are hostile to your suggestions?
   b they are processing the information internally?
   c they don't understand you?

3 When your negotiating partners have explained their interests, you should:
   a go straight into an explanation of your own interests.
   b ask questions to find out more about their needs.
   c summarize what has been said to check that you have not misunderstood anything.

4 Your negotiating partners say they will tell you their decision about the contract as soon as possible. Do you:
   a thank them and say goodbye?
   b congratulate yourself on a successful meeting?
   c tell them you'll ring them in one week's time to hear their decision?

5 You simply can't reach an agreement with your negotiating partners. Should you:
   a suggest taking a break and then have a brainstorming session to generate new solutions?
   b accept the breakdown in the negotiations?
   c accuse the other side of deliberately trying to block the negotiations?

(((9.7))) **3** You are going to hear a conversation between two people trying to negotiate terms for licensing software.

Esther Gold is the Marketing Manager at a company which produces software for connecting banks to the electronic stock markets. Jan De Witt is a potential client from a bank in Amsterdam. Listen and complete his notes.

<u>Trial period</u>
how long?
demo or full version?

<u>Licence agreement</u>
cost?
one-off fee?
discount for multiple copies?
charge for upgrades?

<u>Customization</u>
possible?
cost?

<u>Purchase and delivery</u>
order via fax?
delivery when?
contract need to be signed beforehand?

<u>References</u>
contact numbers of other users?

4 Listen to the conversation again. Find the expressions Jan uses to:

1 state the reason for the phone call
2 enquire about the purchasing procedure
3 change the focus to cost
4 return back to what he was saying before
5 signal that this is his last question
6 show that he has finished with all his enquiries.

5 You are going to negotiate the of terms and conditions of an employment contract. Student A look at File 8 on page 110. Student B, turn to File 17 page 114. Use the language from **4** to help you.

EMAIL

Being clear and brief

 Discuss the questions below.

1 Can you think of examples of emails you have misinterpreted in the past? Compare with a partner.
2 Make a list of reasons why you sometimes find emails difficult to read or easy to misunderstand.
3 Do you ever use smileys (emoticons)? When are they appropriate? Do you know what the following mean? Compare with a partner before checking the key on page 107.

1 :-)   4 :-D

2 ;-)   5 :-(

3 :-|| 6 :-V

 Look at the list you made for ❶ above. Work with a partner and discuss how you can make emails easier to read and understand.

Then look at the cybertips below. Are any of the ideas similar to yours?

CYBERTIP

Being succinct

✦ Put the subject of the email in the subject line, then there is no need to introduce the subject in the message itself.

✦ Communicate the main message right at the beginning. Put your ideas in a logical order.

✦ Break up long sentences into shorter ones. Limit each sentence to one idea.

✦ Use short paragraphs (maximum three sentences). They are easier to understand. Long paragraphs are also hard to track with the scrollbar.

✦ Include only essential information. Cut words, sentences, and even paragraphs that don't contribute.

✦ Avoid formal verbose expressions – where possible use *please* + the imperative.

e.g. *You are requested to acknowledge this email.* = *Please acknowledge this email.*

✦ Avoid impersonal expressions; use adverbs and modal verbs (*need, must, can*, etc.) instead:

e.g *It is probable that she will go.* = *She will probably go.*

It is necessary that I have the report. = *I need the report.*

✦ Only use acronyms and abbreviations (e.g. *rgds, tx, asap*) if you are sure you know what they mean and you know the person well that you are writing to.

✦ To avoid ambiguity, when referring to dates always write the month in full, e.g. *2 July 2010*.
Note that in US English, *2.7* means *7 February*.

✦ Always check through your email before sending it, both for spelling and content.

3 Using the tips, rewrite these extracts from emails to make them more concise.

1

With reference to your email dated Monday 10 March, I have pleasure in enclosing herewith a copy of my CV which gives more details of my qualifications and practical experience. I would be very happy to send you some further information, should it be required, therefore please do not hesitate to contact me in this regard.

2

As of today's date, the order which was placed with you on 8 March is now seven days overdue for delivery, and, therefore, you are requested to get in touch immediately to let us know the circumstances behind the delay and to give us a firm revised date.

I would be grateful if you could send me an email by the end of the week.

3

Invoice No. 897

You are kindly requested to acknowledge receipt of this email. May we remind you that our terms of trade are 30 days and that goods are supplied on the understanding of payment by the proper time.

May we remind you for the third time that this account is overdue for payment.

It is essential that the necessary steps be taken to settle this account immediately.

4

My apologies for having to cancel our meeting of yesterday. Unfortunately an urgent matter came up which I am afraid I could not avoid. I hope this did not cause you too much inconvenience. I hope to be able to rearrange the meeting within the next two weeks. I will contact you in the future to arrange another date.

Once again my sincere apologies.

4 Another way of making informal messages more concise is to omit pronouns, auxiliary verbs, and articles, and to use abbreviations and acronyms. This is even more common when sending text messages on a mobile phone.

e.g. *Pls write back asap. Tx.* = Please write back as soon as possible. Thanks. *Speak 2U soon.* = I will speak to you soon.

Can you understand these sentences? Rewrite them using full forms.

1 Hope this all makes sense. Atb, Catherine.
2 Re tmrw's meeting, here's the agenda.
3 Told staff about meeting. Rgds Jo
4 Have sent copy of contract. Be in touch tomorrow.
5 Not made any more progress since last spoke.
6 Hi Paolo, any suggestions on how we approach the problem?
7 Nice meeting you last week.
8 Just got yr mail. Be glad to give you more info abt the new product line.

ASC140134 Vegetable Seller (Sabzi-farosh) c.1890 (w/c on paper) (detail) by Wassilij Ivanowitsch Nawasoff (20th century) Royal Asiatic Society, London, UK/Bridgeman Art Library

10 CUSTOMERS

KICK OFF

1 Look at the painting. Is customer service any different today?

2 Decide if the following statements about company websites are true (T) or false (F). Then compare your answers with a partner.

- ☐ **1** Websites should be very specifically targeted to individual markets.
- ☐ **2** Websites only need to be in English.
- ☐ **3** Sites must be written by local people in the target country.
- ☐ **4** Cultural as well as linguistic differences should be considered.
- ☐ **5** Jargon and technology terms must be avoided.
- ☐ **6** Methods of payment may vary from country to country.
- ☐ **7** Consumers must be protected against fraud.
- ☐ **8** It's necessary to adapt images and colours for individual countries.

WORDS AT WORK

Internet terms and compound nouns

1 Read the article about websites opposite. Tick (✓) the points from **2** above which are mentioned. Did you have the same ideas?

2 Look at the common Internet terms below.

spam	virus	password	chatroom	firewall	mailing list
cookie	encryption	hacker	portal	homepage	browser

1 Write definitions of four terms you know.

   e.g. browser – this is a program like Internet Explorer that makes it possible for you to look at and read documents on the Internet.

2 Read your definitions to your partner, who has to guess the word. Then turn to page 158 and check your definitions.

The telephone took thirty-six years to gain 10 million consumers, the VCR took nine years, and the Internet two years.
Architects of the Business Revolution

to rely on (*v*) – to need, be dependent on

to take sth into account – to consider

to fail (*v*) – not to do something

prospect (*n*) – somebody who could become a customer

stork (*n*) – big black and white bird with long legs

emblem (*n*) – a picture or image

disease (*n*) – an illness or infection

ARE WE ALL SPEAKING THE SAME LANGUAGE?

According to Dr Frank Burdett, of the University of Luton, many companies that rely purely on a website to trade internationally are failing to take linguistic and cultural differences sufficiently into account. 'Too many businesses still assume that English is and will always be the international language,' he says. 'But in just four years, the proportion of non-English-speaking Internet users has grown from ten per cent to nearly 50 per cent'.

Dr Burdett believes that too many are failing to follow some simple rules. 'First, when creating a foreign-language website, you should never rely exclusively on automatic translation programs. A native speaker of the language in question must edit the words for style and nuances of the language. Second, remember that the more pages an overseas customer or prospect needs to click through to find their language, the more likely they are to leave your site before you would wish. So address them in their language from page one.'

Cultural as well as linguistic differences must also be considered.

'In the West, the stork is widely used as an emblem of childbirth. In Singapore, it means your mother has died. How you present pictures of people is also important. If your site has an image of people looking you straight in the eye, Japanese surfers could take offence at what they might see as a mark of disrespect'.

The colours you select are also important. Dr Burdett says: 'Red works well in China, where it conveys good fortune. But it's the colour of death in Turkey. If you're targeting women you might be tempted to use pink. But outside the UK and the US, yellow would be a better choice. Or if you're marketing organic food, don't use green in tropical countries, where it represents disease. In Indonesia, in fact, it would mean your product is forbidden.'

'It's important that sites are written by local people for local needs. People even buy different things in different ways depending where they come from. Credit cards are barely used in Germany or Holland, and widely used in the UK and in France, though the French ones have chips in them.'

Listening tip

(((10.1))) ❸

1 Work with a partner. Say the words out loud and mark where you think the stress is, on the first word, e.g. **book**mark, or on the second, e.g. down**load**.

a afternoon	**e** overtake	**i** credit card
b website	**f** newspaper	**j** UK-based
c online	**g** overseas	**k** foreign language
d freelance	**h** deadline	**l** vice-president

2 Compare your answers with another pair. Then listen and check.

❹ Complete the sentences using Internet terms from ❷ opposite. Then work with a partner and take it in turns to ask and answer the questions.

1 Have you ever met anyone in a _____ ? Are you still in contact?

2 Are you subscribed to any _____ (e.g. for financial news or jokes)? Are they useful? How long have you been subscribed?

3 When you log on to your computer in the morning, do you have to use a _____ ? Does anybody else know what it is? Why?

4 What do you think about _____ ? Are they always dangerous people or do they sometimes do useful work? Does your company have _____ in operation to protect against such intruders?

5 Have you ever been the victim of a _____ ? Do you receive much _____ in your email? How can you avoid both these problems?

THE INTERVIEW

QXL

Name: Alex Czajkowski
Position: Marketing Director
Company: QXL.com plc
Field of Business: Online auctions
Head Office: London

1 QXL is an online auction house, which conducts consumer-to-consumer and business-to-consumer auctions in eleven languages. Read through the extract below. What is the key factor in determining the price of items?

Q: How does an online auction work?

A: Basically, the seller puts an item up for sale – or a lot of items, for example five CD players or ten DVDs. The customer comes along to the website and can bid any time of the day that he or she happens to be online. In one version of the auction, the bids go up, and the highest bid gets the item; in another version, they go down.

Q: So you set your own price?

A: And that's where all the excitement really is. You're really in control. You decide what something is worth and the price is determined by demand on that item.

Q: But how does it work? Suppose I'm selling something from France to someone who's in Japan.

A: Well the two parties have to work out how to ship it. But if both parties are within the European Union then QXL provides a customer service for this. In this way all the parties are protected and we can reduce auction fraud.

2 Read the text again and match the expressions on left the with the correct definition on the right.

	a	**b**
1 a lot of items	many items	a collection or set of items for sale
2 bid	offer	price
3 to work out	to find a way	to understand
4 fraud	giving money	deceiving people to get money

(((10.2))) **3** Now you are going to hear about QXL's websites. Listen to Alex Czajkowski and answer the questions.

1 Are all QXL's websites only in English?
2 Which country outside Britain was QXL's first website designed for?

4 Listen again. Are the following true (T) or false (F)?

1 The proportion of non-English-speaking Internet users has grown by 50%.
2 The fastest growth is in English-speaking territories.
3 Alex thinks that English will stay the dominant language on the web.
4 You can see a lot of English on German and Swedish websites.
5 Swedish is used in hip and trendy ways.

dominant (*adj*) – most important or powerful
to pop up (*v*) – (informal) to suddenly appear
hip (*adj*), **trendy** (*adj*) – fashionable
palatable (*adj*) – pleasant or acceptable
pun (*n*) – joke, using words that have more than one meaning

5 Listen again to Alex's answer to the last question in the interview.

1 What was QXL's original name? How was it spelt?

2 Why did the company decide to change the name?

Listening tip

(((10.3))) **6** In natural speech, individual sounds are often 'lost' as words are said quickly together. This means that familiar expressions such as, for example, *Do you want to …?* become 'reduced' to sound more like /dʒu: wɒnæ/.

1 Look at the cartoons below. Try to guess what the situations are and complete the sentences with the missing words, as in the example.

2 Compare with a partner before listening to check. Compare with the tapescript on page 150. Did you recognize the reduced structures?

(((10.4))) **7** Listen to a description of how QXL was originally set up and underline which of the expressions in italics you hear, as in the example.

Well Tim Jackson *is / was*[1] the founder of the company *and / in fact*[2] he started the company back in the Fall of 1997. At *that / the*[3] time he *was / worked*[4] a journalist *at / for*[5] the FT, the *Financial Times* newspaper, specializing in things dealing *on / with*[6] the Internet and high tech in general. *And / Then*[7] he kept on seeing all *these / those*[8] business models coming out *from / of*[9] the States. And finally he said, 'Wow you know, one of these *is going / has got*[10] to make it and one of these *is going / has got*[11] to be successful and I *am going / want*[12] to bring it to the UK and make it happen here in the UK.' *And / So*[13] he chose online auctions.

8 ## Talking point

From his voice do you think the representative of QXL is American or British? Why?

Which native English accents do you find most difficult to understand (e.g. American, Australian, Scottish)? Which regional accents and dialects do you find most difficult to understand in your own country?

The average person speaks at about 125 words per minute, whereas thinking speed is in the region of 500 words per minute.
A Guide to Listening

BUSINESS SKILLS

Complaining and reassuring

1 Discuss the following.

1 What services do you provide for your customers (e.g. call centre, helpline, maintenance, website, corporate hospitality)?

2 Look at the corporate values of the American company Johnson & Johnson in the 1950s. What order of importance would you put them in? Compare ideas with a partner, then check with the key on page 107.
- service to the community
- service to its employees and managers
- service to the customers
- service to its stockholders

(((10.6))) **2** Listen to two customers phoning a helpline and complete the table.

	Caller 1	Caller 2
office features mentioned		
type of problem		
helpline operator's suggestions		

3 Look at the expressions below. Tick (✓) the ones you remember from the conversations in **2**.

Listen again and check your answers.

Introducing the problem
- ☐ I wonder if you can help me.
- ☐ I need some advice about …
- ☐ I'm calling about …

Making suggestions
- ☐ Have you tried ….?
- ☐ Are you sure …?
- ☐ What if I … Would that help?

Offering help
- ☐ What can I do for you?
- ☐ What seems to be the problem?
- ☐ How can I help?

Showing concern
- ☐ How awful.
- ☐ I quite understand.
- ☐ That must be very frustrating.

Complaining
- ☐ This really isn't good enough.
- ☐ I'm not happy at all about this.
- ☐ I'd like to speak to your manager.

Reassuring
- ☐ OK if you leave it with me, I'll …
- ☐ Don't worry; we'll sort it out.
- ☐ I'll make sure it doesn't happen again.

Accepting responsibility and apologizing
- ☐ Oh yes, I'm really sorry about the … .
- ☐ You're quite right, I'm extremely sorry.
- ☐ Yes, absolutely. I completely understand.

Thanking for help given
- ☐ Thanks for your help.
- ☐ Great. Thanks very much.
- ☐ Thank you. You've been really helpful.

The main reasons for customers changing suppliers are: service mistakes 44%; indifference, rudeness, and ill-informed service 34%; and poor response to complaints (17%).
One Stop Customer Care

4 Being polite is essential if you want to resolve problems. How could you make the following conversation more positive and polite?

> A: Hello. Anke Bettemann from Pezcos. It's about the deliveries. Put your manager on the phone, now.
>
> B: I am the manager What do you want?
>
> A: I asked you to send me 60 boxes and you've delivered sixteen.
>
> B: Yeah well, mistakes happen. We've got a lot of people off sick.
>
> A: I know. But listen this is the third wrong delivery. I'm tired of it.
>
> B: Sorry. If you want I'll send someone over with the extra stuff.
>
> A: Yes. OK.
>
> B: OK. Goodbye.

(((10.7))) Now listen to a more positive version and compare it with your conversation.

5 Work in pairs. Read and discuss the following case studies. Decide what positive action the service provider could take to resolve the situation.

Case 1

A hotel guest stayed in a hotel for several weeks because his company was setting up a new office in the town where the hotel was located. He paid the bill on leaving the hotel. and then claimed expenses from his company, which he received. Two months later the hotel manager then realized that due to a computer error, he had undercharged the guest by $4,500.

Case 2

A customer bought a personal organizer at a store. While using it one morning the batteries ran out, and the back-up battery failed to function. The back-up battery had not been installed correctly at the store. She lost some important data as a result. She then went back to store to speak to the manager in order to claim compensation.

Case 3

A couple booked a two-week cruise on a river. Due to heavy rain, the level of the river was too high for the cruise boat to move on the water. The boat had to remain at the quayside for the whole of the holiday. On their return, the couple complained to the tour company as they felt they had not received what was advertised in the brochure. The accommodation and food, etc. were fine but they had also hoped to see the sights along the river.

6 Now roleplay the situations in **5**, using the expressions opposite. When you have finished, turn to the key on page 107 to discover how these true life cases were really resolved.

FILE 10

Unit 1, p12 Ex 4, Student B

1 Hamish McLachlan – your email address is:
   HMcLachlan@compuserve.com
   Your telephone number is: 0044 208 554 0089
2 Aleph Makali – your email address is : a.makali@virgin.net
   Your telephone number is: 00252 897 667 3435

FILE 11

Unit 1, p13 Ex 6.3, Student B

1 Your name is Jan Neuermeyer and you work for a company called Freesoft.
You are going to phone a company called Parkis. You want to speak to Irmin
Schmidt. You want to change Thursday's meeting to the following Monday.
Your phone number is 0035 908 76775. Follow the steps below. Student A
will begin the phone call.

1 Say who you are.
2 Say who you want to speak to.
3 Ask if you can leave a message.
4 Give the message.
5 Conclude the conversation.

2 Your name is Jake Parek. You work for a company called Hevelsonn. You are
going to answer a phone call from a supplier. This person will give you the
email address of their Marketing Manager which you have requested.
Follow the prompts below. You are the first person to talk.

1 Answer the phone appropriately.
2 Ask the caller to wait while you find a pen.
3 Check all the details.
4 Thank the caller.

FILE 12

Unit 2, p23 Ex 8, Student B

You have met Student A on an intensive language course. Try to find out as
much as possible about him / her. Remember to make sure you keep your
conversation balanced and show interest in what your partner is saying.
You have some things in common; what are they?

Name:	Sam Foret
Current job:	Director of computer company
Size of company:	150 employees
Type of company:	established 150 years ago

Location:	based in Paris with offices in all European capitals
Job satisfaction:	very happy, ambitious for future
Working hours:	normal but long when travelling
Education:	degree in Business and Fashion from University in Paris
Countries visited:	most of Europe and several times to India
Interests:	skiing and rock climbing, also like the cinema and eating out
Reason for doing course:	to communicate more confidently with foreign partners
Opinion of course:	fantastic, interested in advanced course
Email address:	foret@kanel.fr

FILE 13

Unit 2, p25 Ex 3, Extended speaking activity – interview questions

1 Describe yourself with three adjectives.
2 What are you most proud of on your CV?
3 Are you married?
4 Are you planning to have any children in the near future?
5 Do you have any particular health problems?
6 Are you a member of any trade unions or political parties?
7 What are some of the things in your current job you have done well?
8 What is the most difficult assignment you have had?
9 What skills and abilities do you have?
10 What steps have you taken to improve your job skills?
11 What is your current salary?
12 Why do you want to leave your current job?
13 How has your job prepared you to take on greater responsibility?
14 Recall an incident where you made a major mistake. What did you do after the mistake was made? What did you learn from this mistake?
15 Are you prepared to travel for work? Would you be prepared to work abroad?

FILE 14

Unit 6, p62 Ex 6, Student B

❶ Student A, who you know quite well, will ring you to arrange a business meeting to finalize a contract. As you listen, make sure you follow the points below – also check you've understood the day:

– check time   – check phone number
– check place   – summarize arrangement

❷ Ring Student A to arrange a visit to the theatre together – the details are below. Tell Student A you have recently changed your phone number and give the new one.

day: Thursday 30th of next month
place: the bar next to the theatre
time: 19.50
new mobile number: 066 754 2876 50

FILE 15

Unit 5, p52 Ex 4, Student B

1 It's the beginning of June. You have just completed a successful piece of work for Student A, (who you know well) which you really enjoyed doing. You are very busy for the next three weeks. The first day you are free is 28 June.

2 You are about to sign a large contract with Student B's company. You want to invite Student B for lunch just to discuss a few last-minute issues you are concerned about. You are busy the rest of this week but next week is free. You want to meet as soon as possible and are prepared to cancel any appointments you have to fit in with Student A.

FILE 16

Unit 7, p73 Ex 9, Student B

1 You have just arrived on flight BA 1676 from Hong Kong. You have lost all your suitcases. You are staying at the McHotel (tel. 898 7766). Student A is an official at the lost luggage office. Do the following:
  a Explain the situation.
  b Give any details required.

2 You are a receptionist. Student A is a guest at your hotel who has just arrived and has room number 55 on the fifth floor (lift down the corridor). Breakfast is served between 07.00 and 10.00. Do the following:
  a Check the guest in.
  b Give any information necessary.

3 You are staying at a hotel. The time is 01.00 in the morning. The light in your bathroom is not working. You want some champagne. Student A is the receptionist at the hotel. Make your requests.

4 You are the receptionist at a hotel in your home town. It's Saturday night. Student A is a guest in your hotel. Answer Student A's questions.

5 You are checking out of your hotel. You have made no phone calls. You haven't consumed anything from the mini bar. You want to pay by credit card. Student A is the hotel receptionist. Do the following:
  a Ask for the bill.   b Query the bill.   c Answer any questions.

FILE 17

Unit 9, p93 Ex 5, Student B

You have just been offered the post of Press Officer at the International Head Office of a large bank. You are negotiating the terms of your contract with Student A, the Human Resources Manager. You really want to accept this senior position; however, there are at least two points you are not prepared to compromise on. Before you begin, spend a few minutes deciding which terms you think should take priority (including the two you will not compromise on) and what you are going to say.

- three months' probationary period
- permanent contract
- basic salary of $150,000 p.a.
- performance-related annual bonus
- company car plus petrol allowance

- 30 days holiday p.a.
- mortgage at 1% interest
- possibility of profit-share scheme in the future

FILE 18

Unit 10, p101 Ex 7, Student B

You have a budget of $60,000 to spend on some of the features of this futuristic home. Student A is a salesperson and will explain what the features can do and how much they cost. Before you begin your discussion with Student A, decide which features you like (remember you cannot spend more than $60,000). If Student A tries to convince you to buy something you don't want you can use expressions like:

I don't need this because ...
I can't have this because ...

KEY

- **microwave** $4,000

- **rubbish bin** $500

- **robot** $37,000

- **smart VCR** $3,500

- **fridge** $4,100

- **mobile phone** $3,200

- **central audio / video control** $5,500

- **lighting, music, and temperature** $10,000

- **view changer** $8,000

- **teletransporter** $40,000

MBI

Possible areas of contention	Current situation at MBI	What you know about Fonekom	Option 1	Option 2
Head Office	New York	Brussels	must keep head office in New York	move to California
CEO	Pat Bellusci 55 years old, several previous highly prestigious CEO positions at multinationals	Andrea Poitier 35 years old, no previous CEO experience, major risk taker, very ambitious	Bellusci becomes new CEO – with Poitier as second in command	Bellusci becomes new CEO. Poiter offered massive pay-off
Image	long-established reputation for reliability and value for money, well known throughout the world	creative, innovative but new to the field	retain established MBI image, but introduce Fonekom logo into MBI's logo and call the new company MBIF	call new company MBI.kom and make the image more funky (though at risk of losing some big customers)
Management culture	hierarchical structure, formal but effective supervision system	flat structure, very informal style no controls	keep present hierarchy but with less formality	use the opportunity to restructure the company and change its culture
Working conditions – salaries, bonuses working hours	monthly salaries indexed to inflation bonuses for senior managers fixed working hours high turnover of staff	unknown not known	maintain current situation	Fonekom manages to attract and retain very good staff – adopt their system
Fringe benefits	company cars long holidays luncheon vouchers free phone calls for all employees free use (including family members) of company's massive leisure centre	shares in the company	maintain current MBI situation	cut costs by reducing some of these benefits

1 Comparisons

1 Many adjectives use *more* and *the most* for the comparative and superlative form.

e.g. *more intelligent > the most intelligent*
more useful >the most useful

The exceptions to this are all adjectives of one syllable (see table below), and adjectives that end in -y or -ow.

e.g. *easy > easier > the easiest*
happy > happier > the happiest
narrow > narrower > the narrowest
yellow > yellower > the yellowest

Most 1-syllable adjectives *small, great*	Comparative + *er* *smaller, greater*	Superlative + *est* *the smallest, the greatest*
1 vowel + 1 consonant *big, wet*	double final consonant + *er* *bigger, wetter*	double final consonant + *est* *the biggest, wettest*

Note also the following irregular adjectives:

Adjective	Comparative	Superlative
good	*better*	*the best*
bad	*worse*	*the worst*
little	*less*	*the least*
much	*more*	*the most*
far	*further / farther*	*the furthest / farthest*

2 To compare two people, things, or events use a comparative adjective + *than*.
*Microsoft is **bigger than** Amazon.*
*A Ferrari is **more expensive than** a Fiat.*

3 To make an equal comparison (to say that things are the same), you can use *as … as*.
*Canada's GDP per head is **as big as** Italy's.*
*Sweden's inflation rate is not **as low as** Japan's.*

4 To compare adverbs (you usually make adverbs by adding ly to the verb, e.g. *slow > slowly*) use *more* and *less*.
*I work **more efficiently** if I remember to take short breaks.*

5 Comparisons can be made stronger or weaker by using modifiers such as: *a lot, a little, considerably, much, slightly*.
*This one is **much / slightly / a lot bigger than** that one.*

A Form the comparative and superlative of the following adjectives.

1 fast	**4** late	**7** far
2 cheap	**5** good	**8** happy
3 fat	**6** bad	**9** feasible

B Read this report comparing the use of online investment facilities in Canada and the US. Underline the correct form in italics.

Nearly half (48%) of Canadian Internet users who have been online for less *than / that* [1] a year have already banked online, while just 13% of American Internet newcomers have done so. Active Internet users in Canada and the United States who have not yet banked online agreed they favour *more / most* [2] traditional methods of banking and have concerns about privacy or security.

15% of active Canadian Internet users have invested online compared to 10% of American users. In both Canada and the United States, the *bigger / biggest* [3] users of online banking are aged 18 to 34. Internet users aged 55 and older are *less / the least* [4] likely to do their finances over the web.

Clearly the use of online banking and investing will only increase in the future as the *younger / youngest* [5] generation, who are the *more / most* [6] comfortable using the web for these purposes, ages and moves into *more / most* [7] complex financial dealings.

While Canadians are *more / most* [8] likely to take their finances online, active Internet users in the United States are far more *likely / likelier* [9] to shop online *than / as* [10] Canadian Internet users, and subscribe to three times *as / so* [11] many online newsletters *than / as* [12] their Canadian counterparts. For example, *more / most* [13] American Internet users (77%) have bought a product or service online *than / as* [14] Canadian Internet users (68%). In the last year, American online shoppers have made more than twice as many online buys *as / that* [15] Canadians – 14 purchases compared to 6.5.

2 Conditionals

1 First conditional

if + present simple + *will*

We use this form to say what we believe the result will be of a future action.

> *If you **don't finish** the report by lunchtime, the boss won't be pleased.*

It is often used in negotiations to state conditions.

> *If **you order** more than ten, **we'll give** you a discount.*

It is also used for threats and warnings.

> ***You'll get** an electric shock if **you touch** that.*

You can use **unless** to mean 'if not' in the condition clause.

> *You'll miss the flight **unless** you leave immediately.*

2 Second conditional

if + past simple + *would*

We use this form to talk about future situations that we don't think are likely to happen or are imaginary.

> *If **I behaved** like that, the boss **would sack** me.*
> (But I never have behaved in this way in the past and it's very unlikely I will start now.)

> *If **I were** the CEO of the company, **I would** completely restructure it.*
> (But I am not, and never will be.)

Compare this with a real possiblity, which would be expressed in the first conditional.

> *If I **don't get** promoted, I **will probably leave** the company.*

We use the second conditional in negotiations to make tentative offers, or when we want to show we are not sure about the situation or are less willing to make a concession.

> ***Would you accept** my offer if **I agreed** to lower the price by 1%?*
> (I am not sure this will be acceptable to you; 1% may not be enough.)

The second conditional is also used to make a request sound more polite.

> ***Would you mind** if **we postponed** the meeting till tomorrow?*

NB In conditional sentences we can change the order of the 'if' clause and the main clause.

> *I'll help you **if** you want. / **If** you want, I'll help you.*
> *I wouldn't work here **if** the salary wasn't so good. / **If** the salary … , I wouldn't work here.*

A Match the beginnings with appropriate endings.

1 If I bought that many
2 If I go to my English lesson today
3 If I had time
4 If I have time
5 If I passed the exam
6 So if I buy in bulk

a I will finish the report today.
b I will get a discount.
c I will learn more words.
d I would be very happy.
e I would spend too much.
f I would study more.

B Underline the correct form.

1 If you *press / will press* too hard, it *will / would* break.
2 I *will / would* tell her if I *see / will see* her.
3 If I *am / were* CEO I *will / would* float the company.
4 I *worked / would work* in London if I *had / would have* the chance.
5 I *will / would* buy a new house if I *win / won* the lottery.

C Put the verbs in brackets into appropriate tenses and then complete the sentences.

1 If my boss (*ask*) me to do some overtime today, I … .
2 I probably (*get*) promoted if … .
3 If my company (*ask*) me to study English for a month in London, I … .
4 I (*be*) more relaxed at work if … .
5 If I (*can*) live anywhere in the world I … .

3 Countable and uncountable nouns

1 Countable nouns are things we can count. They can be made plural using an *s* and can be preceded by *a / an / one*.
   e.g. *a book, one book, two books*
   a plan, one plan, several plans

2 Uncountable nouns are things we cannot count. They **cannot** be made plural using an *s* and **cannot** be preceded by *a / an / one*. They are often materials, liquids, and abstract things.
   e.g. *water, gold, health*

3 Some words may be uncountable in English but countable in other languages.

e.g. *accommodation, advertising, advice*

In some cases (e.g. *business, experience, glass, paper*) nouns can be both countable or uncountable depending on their use.

***Paper** is becoming an expensive commodity.*

*She reads **the paper** (i.e. newspaper) every day.*

4 You can use *some* with plural countable and uncountable nouns.

*There **are some** new computers in the stockroom. (C)*

*There **is some** new information about the problem. (U)*

We use *some* in questions with both plural countable and uncountable nouns when the question is an offer or request (when we can see what it is that we want and know it is there).

*Would you like **some** beer / advice / information? (U)*

*Can you give me **some** books? (C) (I can see the books I want on the shelf.)*

5 *Any* is used in questions with both plural countable and uncountable nouns to ask if something is available or if it exists.

*Do you have **any** books on the subject? (C) (I don't know if you have any books.)*

*Is there **any** beer left? (U)*

We use *any* in negative statements with both plural countable and uncountable nouns to express the idea of nothing.

*We don't have **any** plans. (C)*

*There isn't **any** money. (U)*

6 The table on the right shows some of quantifiers you can use with countable and uncountable nouns.

quantifier	use
many	with countable nouns in questions and negatives (for positive statements use *a lot of*) e.g *How many people are there in your department? Not many.*
much	with uncountable nouns in questions and negatives (for positive statements use *a lot of*) *How much time have you got? Not much.*
lots of / a lot	with countable and uncountable nouns in negative and positive statements *There are a lot of people in the department and we have got lots of time for this project. We don't have a lot of (much) money, though.*
a few / few	with countable nouns *A few letters of my friends are coming.* (means 'a small number', but is neutral or positive) *Few people came to the meeting.* (means 'not many' and is negative)
a little / little	with uncountable nouns *We have spent a little of the money already.* (means a small amount, but is neutral or positive) *You have little chance of succeeding.* (means 'not much' and is negative)

A Write countable (C) or uncountable (U) after the following nouns.

1 baggage		**7** help	
2 behaviour		**8** insurance	
3 suggestion		**9** job	
4 evidence		**10** idea	
5 function		**11** merchandise	
6 furniture		**12** news	

B Underline the correct form.

The Internet search engines are *some / any* [1] of the largest and most commonly used search engines on the World Wide Web. Their huge databases of millions of web pages typically index *each / every* [2] word on *each / every* [3] one of these pages. By using them, searchers hope to find *every / all* [4] page that contains an occurrence of their search term.

Several / Enough [5] search engine companies have boasted for years of the millions of pages indexed in their database, and *much / many* [6] others gladly announce the latest total number of pages, or URLs, in their database. However, not *all / every* [7] search engines can actually deliver the total number of results that they claim to find, and for the moment there aren't *any / some* [8] that can make really intelligent searches which always find what the searcher was looking for. Despite this, most generate *enough / several* [9] information for the general public – but for serious researchers this may be too *little / few* [10].

4 Future forms

There are three main forms which we use to talk about the future.

1 *be + going to* + infinitive

We use *be + going to* to refer to plans and intentions which we decided before the time of speaking.

> *He's going to change job next year.* (He has already decided to do this.)
> *Are you going to see the Louvre while you're in Paris?* (Is this part of your planned itinerary?)

We also use this form to make predictions based on present or past evidence. In some cases we can already see that something is starting to happen.

> *Look – it's going to rain.* (The clouds are black.)
> *They're not going to like these changes to the schedules.* (Past experience shows they don't like changes.)

2 Present continuous

We use the present continuous to talk about personal plans and arrangements in a very specific way, particularly when we mention the time and place.

> *I am meeting Catriona at 4.30.*
> *They're flying on Wednesday.*

Compare:

> *We are opening a new office in New York next year.* (We have already started looking for premises.)
> *We are going to open a new office in New York one day.* (This is only an intention, no plans have been made yet.)

3 *will* + infinitive

We use this form to express a spontaneous decision or an offer to do something made at the moment of speaking.

> *The phone's ringing. OK I'll answer it.*
> *I've lost my wallet. I'll help you find it.*

In emails and letters we use *will* to refer to attachments or say what action we intend to take.

> *As you will see from the attached copy …*
> *I'll contact our sales manager and ask her to mail you.*
> *I'll be in touch soon.*

We also use the *will* form to make predictions based on personal intuitions (rather than visible evidence).

> *Interest rates will probably go down if the Democrats win the election.*
> *I'm sure England won't win the World Cup.*

The *will* form is also used to talk about future states and events with verbs that don't take the present continuous.

> *She will be 30 next May.*
> *We will know tomorrow.*

A Underline the most appropriate form of the verb in italics. In some cases more than one may be possible.

The year is 2097 and some space scientists from around the world are meeting to discuss what they have already prepared for future projects.

'We *are preparing / will prepare* [1] to send a rocket to Pluto,' announced the Americans. 'It *is having / will have* [2] six men aboard and *is staying / will stay* [3] for a whole month before making the long trip back to Earth.'

'That's nothing!' said the Russians. 'Next week we *are launching / are going to launch* [4] our spaceship containing 200 men and women to Uranus. We *will probably start / are probably going to start* [5] a colony there.'

'Our country *is beating / will beat* [6] you both,' said the British scientist. 'We *will / are going to send* [7] a rocket straight to the Sun.'

'How *are you going to do / are you doing* [8] that?' said the American and Russian scientists. 'The rocket *is going to / will melt* [9] before it gets there.' 'No, it *isn't / won't* [10],' replied the British scientist. 'We *will / are going to* [11] send it up at night.'

B Complete the sentences using *will*, *going to*, or the present continuous of the verb in brackets.

1 'Could I speak to Mr Yo, please?' 'Yes of course, I … (*fetch him*)
2 I'm afraid I can't come to the office dinner next week because I … (*go on holiday*)
3 We've finally made a decision about the product launch. We … (*go ahead May*)
4 'We're running out of envelopes.' ' I … (*order more*)
5 'The photocopier doesn't work.' 'OK. I …' (*call engineer*)
6 He's resigned from the company and he … (*take job in New York*)

C Underline the correct form on the basis of the comment in brackets below.

1 We *will sell / are selling* the company. (We've found a buyer.)

2 I will meet / am meeting Jo at the airport.
(Jo knows about this arrangement.)

3 I will help / am helping her.
(I've just decided.)

4 Shares in BMX will / are going to fall.
(I have some inside information.)

5 Jo is going to teach / is teaching me Chinese.
(Our lessons have already begun.)

5 The gerund and the infinitive after verbs

There are some verbs which are always followed by by the gerund or *ing* form, and others which are followed by the infinitive with *to*.

There are some rules that can help you work out these verb patterns.

1 The gerund

We use the *ing* form:

a after verbs and expressions of emotional attitude towards something, e.g. *like, love, dislike, enjoy, hate, stand, mind*.
Working Americans **enjoy spending** time with their families.

b after certain other verbs, e.g. *risk, avoid, spend time*.
I don't want to **risk losing** their custom.

c when the activity is the subject or object of a sentence.
Using a computer all day can be bad for your back.
We don't encourage **drinking** on the premises.

d after verbs that express ideas or advice, e.g. *recommend, propose, suggest*.
Health experts **recommend taking** much longer lunch breaks.
(Also *The experts* **recommend** *that* **we take** *longer breaks*.)

e We also use the gerund immediately after prepositions e.g. *before, after, since, by, about, on, for, in, to*.
An MP3 is generally used **for listening** to music.
Before using it you need to attach the headphones.
I look forward **to hearing** from you.

2 The infinitive

We use the infinitive:

a after verbs that focus on a purpose or objective e.g. *would like, want, plan, promise, decide, hope*.
We **would like to inform** you that we have **decided to accept** your proposal.

b after verbs that tell someone what they can do or what we want them to do, e.g. *allow, ask, enable, expect, help, instruct, permit, persuade, tell*.
This program **allows** you **to write** spreadsheets.
I **persuaded** him **to let** me use his mobile.

c as the subject of the sentence to indicate an objective.
To learn English (objective) you need to study hard.
Compare with: **Learning** English (activity) is easy.

d after adjectives and with *how*.
It's **easy to use**.
If you like I'll show you **how to use** one.

Some verbs take either the *ing* form or the infinitive depending on their meaning.

I **stopped to look** at the website. (I interrupted what I was doing before.)
I **stopped looking** at the website when the boss came in. (I was looking at the website before he came in.)

A Underline the correct form.

FAQ (frequently asked questions): Document that answers the most common questions in a newsgroup or mailing list. It may be a good idea *studying / to study* [1] the FAQ document before *posing / to pose* [2] a question to a mailing list or newsgroup in order to avoid *repeating / to repeat* [3] a common question.

log on: This term means *connecting / to connect* [4] to a computer *gaining / to gain* [5] access to its programs or information. Often this is done by *writing / to write* [6] one's user identity and password.

B Put the verbs in italics into the *-ing* form or the infinitive.

A company thought it would help *continue* [1] its perfect safety record by *show* [2] its workers a film aimed at *encourage* [3] the use of safety goggles while *work*.[4] Unfortunately the film's depiction of industrial accidents was so graphic that 25 workers suffered minor injuries when they were trying *leave* [5] the screening room. Thirteen others fainted and one man required seven stitches after *cut* [6] his head when he fell off a chair while *watch* [7] the film.

6 Link words

1 Meaning

a Link words used for ordering and sequencing include:
informal or neutral: *first, then, next, at the same time, finally, in the end*
formal: *firstly, secondly, simultaneously, subsequently, lastly*

b Link words used for adding information include:
informal or neutral: *and, also, too, besides, what is more, as well*
formal: *moreover, in addition, furthermore*

c Link words used for contrasting include:
informal or neutral: *although, though, even though however, despite this, instead, on the other hand, even so, then again*
formal: *by contrast, nevertheless, on the contrary, nonetheless, conversely*

d Link words used for correcting or giving different emphasis to previous statement include:
informal or neutral: *actually, in fact*
formal: *as a matter of fact, in reality*

e Link words used for giving parallel, informal or neutral information: *again, in the same way, similarly, equally* formal: *by the same token, likewise*

f Link words used for giving examples and specifying include:
informal or neutral: *such as, like, this means that*
formal: *for example (e.g.), for instance, that is to say, i.e.*

g Link words used for indicating a result include:
informal or neutral: *so, consequently, as a result*
formal: *therefore, thus, hence, thereby, accordingly*

h Link words used for concluding include:
informal or neutral: *to conclude*
formal: *in conclusion, in summary*

2 Word order

Most of the words and expressions above can appear at the beginning or in the middle of the sentence. Many writers follow them with a comma.

*We have lost our main customer. **As a result**, we will have to make some drastic cuts.*
*You have shown no initiative. **In addition**, your work has been of substandard quality.*
*We will, **however**, still require 600 copies of the CD ROM.*
*We have **thus** decided to cancel our order.*

Too and *as well* are generally found at the end of the sentence.
*She has been to Paris and to Berlin **too / as well**.*
although, though, and *even though* can be placed in two positions.
***Although** he has worked here for years he has never been promoted.*
*He has never been promoted **even though** he has worked here for years.*

A Underline the most appropriate word or expression in italics. Check with a dictionary if you are not sure of the exact differences in meaning between words.

1 I still remember my first day at work. *Similarly / On the other hand* I can't remember anything at all about my first project.
2 I don't think she's ever been to New York. *In addition / fact* I don't think she's ever been to the US.
3 I have worked in Asia. I have *also / too* worked in the Middle East.
4 We have still not received payment for our invoice. *As well / Moreover*, the contract for the current order has still not been signed.
5 She doesn't speak Japanese very well. *However / On the contrary*, she speaks Chinese fluently.

B Complete the extract from the report using these words:
also, although, consequently, finally, however, moreover

Sales are running at a lower rate than last year. _____ ¹ stocks have grown. _____ ², the general decline in the steel industry has meant that there have _____ ³ been job losses. _____ ⁴, this trend may be offset by the growth in new technologies involving steel, _____ ⁵ we may not see the results of this for several years. _____ ⁶, the appointment of the new sales manager …

7 Modals

Modal verbs are auxiliary verbs – they are usually used in a sentence with another main verb. We use them to express concepts such as ability, advice, obligation, necessity, and possiblity. We also use them in offers, requests, and suggestions.

Form
Modals have no s in the third person singular.
e.g. She **should** study more.
     He **might** give the presentation.

Modals do not use the auxiliary verb do / does to make questions and negatives (because modal verbs are auxiliary verbs themselves).
e.g. He **can't** come tomorrow. **Shall** I help you?

Modals do not usually have a past or future form. This means that a different verb often needs to be used when expressing past or future ideas.
e.g. I **can't** do it today and I **won't be able** to do it tomorrow.
     You **must** work harder! We **had to** work very hard last year.

1 Ability, possibility: *can, could, may,* and *might*

Use can(not) to express a general ability to do something.
     She **can't** speak English very well.
     I **can** play golf.

Use can to express certainty (when something is 100% possible) and cannot (can't) to express 100% impossibility.
     I **can** come tomorrow. (I am certain.)
     She **cannot** come to the meeting. (It is impossible for her to come.)

Use may and might (not) in situations when you are not certain. Might is usually less definite than may.
     I **may / might** come to the meeting. (It is possible that I will come, but it's not definite.)

You can also use may, might, and could to speculate about the future or talk about probability.
     We **may** decide to open a new office in Warsaw. (50% probability)
     They **might** not come to the meeting if they don't have enough time. (Less than 50% probability)
     I **could** be wrong. (but not necessarily)
     Interest rates **could / might** even go up by another 5%. (I am speculating.)

A Underline the correct form.

1 We *will / may* go the US next year but I'm not sure.
2 In five years' time inflation *will / could* be at over 15%.
3 I *will / may* tell him as soon as I see him.
4 It *could / will* rain, so we should take our umbrellas.

B Complete these sentences about your work environment using *can (not)* and *may / might not.*

1 I _____ arrive and leave at a certain time.
2 I _____ get a rise in salary this year.
3 I _____ eat while working.
4 I _____ play music while I work.
5 I _____ take frequent coffee breaks.
6 I _____ play the piano.
7 I _____ look for a new job in the next few years.
8 I _____ wear whatever I want.

2 Advice and obligation: *have to, must, need,* and *should*

When we tell someone that we think something would be good or useful for them we use *should*, and *must* when we want to give them a very strong recommendation.
     You **should** try using another search engine – it would be much quicker. You **must** go and see that movie – you would love it.

We use should when ethics are involved.
     I think the Third World debt **should** be cancelled.
     Companies **should** give more of their profits to charity.

When talking about our general work responsibilities (to show that an obligation probably comes from some one else) we use *have to*. When we want to say that something is not necessary or is not our responsibility we use *don't have to* or *don't need to*.
     We **have to** arrive before nine in the morning but we **don't have** to clock in.
     Although I work in Finland I **don't need / have** to use Finnish in my job because everyone speaks English.

We tend to use have to and not must when giving instructions – must sounds impolite.
Alternatively we use the imperative (with *please*).
     Please **visit** our website where you will find details of all our prices.

We use *must* when we give ourselves orders. *Must* is also found in warnings and notices.

> I **must** answer all those emails.
> We **must** get ourselves a new filing system.
> Helmets **must** be worn on the building site at all times.

We use *must not* to prohibit something.

> You **mustn't** smoke in a non-smoking compartment.

A Underline the correct form in italics.

1 We *don't have to / mustn't* work tomorrow because it's a public holiday.
2 You *don't have to / mustn't* touch that. It will give you an electric shock.
3 We generally *have to / must* be at work before 09.30.
4 You *have to / must* visit this website. It's really interesting.
5 You *have to / should* try this new version; it's much more reliable.

B Compare these sentences about your own work environment using *(don't) have to*, *must(n't)*, *should(n't)*, or *(don't) need*. Try to use each form at least once.

1 I _____ contact clients by phone.
2 I _____ go on specialization courses.
3 I _____ go to frequent meetings.
4 I _____ make written reports of my work progress.
5 I _____ spend several hours a week studying English.
6 I _____ travel frequently for work.
7 I _____ use the Internet for my own personal use.

3 Offers, requests, invitations, and suggestions: *can, may, could, would, shall,* and *will*

Use *can, may,* and *shall* to **offer** to do something. *May* is more formal.

> **May / Can / Shall** I help you?

Use *can, could, will* and *would* to **request** something. *could* and *would* are more polite.

> **Can / Could / Will / Would** you help me?

Use *would you like* to **invite** someone.

> **Would you like** to come out for dinner tonight?

Use *shall* to make a **suggestion**.

> **Shall** I open the window?
> **Shall** we go to the bar?

Make offers, invitations, and requests using the prompts.

1 You need to send a fax.
2 You need a taxi.
3 You want to know if you can smoke.
4 At lunch, you can't understand the menu.
5 Invite a client to dinner.
6 Offer to help client with his luggage.
7 Suggest having a break.
8 You want the bill.
9 You need help with your luggage.
10 You want to know when breakfast is served.

8 Numbers, dates, and measurements

1 Cardinal and ordinal numbers

213	*two hundred and thirteen* (UK)
	two hundred thirteen (US)
2,130,362	*two million, one hundred and thirty thousand, three hundred and sixty-two*
13th	*thirteenth*
31st	*thirty-first*

2 Calendar dates

UK: day / month / year – 10.03.01
the tenth of March, two thousand and one
or *March (the) tenth, two thousand and one*

US: month / day / year – 03.10.01
October third, two thousand one

1996
nineteen ninety six
or *nineteen hundred and ninety six*

1701
seventeen oh one
or *seventeen hundred and one*

3 Fractions, decimals, percentages

1/4	*a quarter / one quarter*
1/2	*a half / one half*
3/4	*three quarters*
0.25	*(zero) point two five*
0.056	*zero point zero five six*
37.9	*thirty seven point nine*
10%	*ten per cent*
100%	*one hundred per cent*

4 Money

€678	six hundred and seventy-eight euros
€1.50	one euro fifty (cents)
$450,617	four hundred fifty thousand six hundred and seventeen dollars
$1.90	one dollar ninety

5 Measurements

1 m 70	one metre seventy
3.5 kg	three point five kilos
3 m x 6 m	three metres by six
10°	ten degrees
–10°	minus ten degrees or ten degrees below zero

6 Sport

| 3-0 | three nil (football) |
| 30-0 | thirty love (tennis) |

7 Phone numbers

0044 161 980 4166	zero zero four four one six one nine eight zero four one double six
	or oh oh four four …, etc.
ext. 219	extension two one nine
0800	oh eight hundred

Write down the following information about yourself and then find out the same information about your partner. Take it in turns to ask questions.

e.g. *When did you get your first job?*

1 The date you got your first or current job.
2 Your weight in kilos when you were eighteen.
3 Your ideal temperature for a summer's day.
4 The price of a square metre of flat / house space in your town.
5 The percentage of your day that you spend on the phone.
6 Your home telephone number.
7 The name and email of a friend.
8 What you think the ratio of work to leisure should be.
9 The ideal length of a business lunch.

9 Passive form

Correct form of *be* + past participle

1 We use the passive:

a when we are more interested in the person or object that experiences an action than the person or object that performs the action.
*The New York stock exchange **was founded** in 1792.* (The stock exchange is the most important element in this sentence, the identity of the person who founded it is irrelevant.)

b when we don't know or cannot express who or what performed the action.
*Four hundred thousand credit cards **are stolen** every year.* (We don't know exactly who steals the cards.)
*The photocopier **was left** on all night.* (We don't know who was the last person to use it.)

c to describe processes. We use *by* to say who or what performs the action.
*The chemicals **are transported** by lorry and **are then delivered** to the factory.*

d to report formal decisions or to make announcements.
*It **has been decided** to lay off 1,000 workers.*
*It **was agreed** to spread the redundancies over six months.*

2 Verbs often used in the passive:

a to describe processes: *is transported / is collected / is transferred / is analysed*

b to describe creation and discovery: *was produced / was invented / was discovered*

c to describe damage and injury: *was harmed / was damaged / was killed*

3 We don't use the passive when:

a we want to be more informal, e.g. in emails and spoken English.
*A **comparison was made** of the two products.* (formal, scientific)
***We compared** the two products.* (neutral, spoken English)

b it is important to be direct and easy to understand, e.g. in manuals and instructions.
*It is essential that the **disk drive unit is switched on** before use.* (indirect)
*Make sure **you switch on** the disk drive unit before using it.* (direct)

A Underline the correct form in italics.

1 Fifty thousand copies *sold / were sold* last year.
2 He *has promoted / has been promoted*.
3 They *have promoted / have been promoted* the movie all over the world.
4 It *decided / was decided* that the service *should discontinue / should be discontinued*.
5 The inflation rate *is / has* gone up.
6 He *is / has* bought himself a car.
7 Your taxi *is / has* arrived.
8 She *was / had* taken to the airport.
9 The machine *was / had* stopped for repairs.
10 An important document *had lost / had been lost*.

B Put the verbs in italics into the active or passive form of the past simple.

An incredible mistake *occur*[1] in a hospital. A nurse *notice*[2] that many of their dying patients had one thing in common: they had all stayed in same room in intensive care. A team *bring*[3] in to investigate the possible causes, and many precautionary measures *take*[4]: the room *fumigate*[5]; the air conditioning unit *check*[6]; and all medical equipment serviced. More patients died and criminal involvement of some kind *suspect*[7]. The doctors *decide*[8] to monitor the room even more closely. What they discovered late that night was that a cleaner *come*[9] into the ward every night with an electric floor polishing machine. There was only one electric socket in this ward, however, and she therefore *unplug*[10] the life support system each night in order to provide power for her polisher, obviously without thinking about the terrible consequences.

C Complete the second sentence so that it means the same as the first.

1 Your email has been forwarded to the Marketing Department.
   I have …
2 The form should be completed in black ink.
   Please …
3 An analysis was carried out of the samples.
   We …
4 The following points should be borne in mind when dealing with complaints.
   Remember …

10 Past simple

infinitive + *ed*

For irregular verbs, see page 134.

We use the past simple to talk about completed actions in the recent past (even one second ago) or the distant past.
> She **founded** the company in 1969.
> They **went** to the bar a few minutes ago.

If you say **when** something happened (e.g. *yesterday, last week, when she was at university, many years ago*) you must use the past simple and not the present perfect.

Time expressions which are typically associated with the past simple are: *yesterday, last night, a few minutes ago, in 1945, then, before, after.*

11 Past continuous

was / were + verb + *ing*

1 We use the past continuous to describe an event that was in progress when it was interrupted by a shorter event. The past simple is used for the shorter completed event.
   > I **met** Jo when I **was coming** to work.
   > While I **was surfing** the Internet the boss **walked** in.

   It also describes an event that was in progress around a particular past time.
   > What **were you doing** at 4.00 p.m.?
   > I **was taking** part in a meeting.

   We can use the past continuous to make tentative suggestions or requests.
   > I **was wondering** if you could help me with a problem?
   > I **was thinking** about taking next week off.

2 The past continuous is not used to talk about past habits or to refer to how often something happened.
   > We **didn't sell** many products in our first years of business.
   > I **phoned** them several times yesterday.

A Underline the correct form in italics.

1 I *slept / was sleeping* when the fire alarm *went / was going* off.
2 A: Then we went to the pub.
   B: What *did you do / were you doing* after that?
3 We *did / were doing* business with them on a few occasions.

4 They *lived / were living* in Paris first, then Bonn and then they *moved / were moving* to Prague.

B Underline the correct tense in italics on the basis of the information in the sentence below.

1 I didn't know he *used / was using* Powerpoint.
(I didn't know he knew how to use Powerpoint.)
2 I *left / was leaving* the room when my boss came in.)
(I probably didn't want to see my boss.)
3 As I *told / was telling* you yesterday.
(I probably have something more to tell you.)
4 They asked me what I *did / was doing*.
(They wanted to know what my job was.)

12 Past perfect

had + past participle

1 We use the past perfect when we are already talking about the past and we want to talk about an earlier past.
*When I **arrived** at the casino I realized I **had lost** my keys.*

We don't use the past perfect when we describe simultaneous or sequential events.
*I **lost** my keys when I **went** to the casino.*

2 Certain time expressions are typically associated with the past perfect. They are used when one completed action happened before another.
e.g. *by, by the time that, when, as soon as, before, after.*
*The meeting **had already started** when I arrived.*
*After he **had discussed** the current projects he went on to talk about future plans.*

A Underline the correct form in italics.

1 I *saw / had seen* his presentation before so I *didn't want / hadn't wanted* to see it again.
2 I *left / had left* an MP3 for repair – is it ready yet?
3 We *explained / had explained* that the special offer *finished / had finished*.
4 I *thought / had thought* that I *told / had told* you already.

B Underline the correct tense in italics on the basis of the information in the sentence below.

1 I remembered that Jo *worked / had worked* for IBM.
(Jo doesn't work for IBM now.)
2 I realized the boss *was / had been* in the next room.
(I could hear the boss's voice.)
3 They asked me if I *came / had come* from Beijing.
(They wanted to know about my journey.)
4 When her husband *left / had left* for work she phoned her mother.
(She often phoned her mother.)

C Put the verbs in italics into the past simple, past perfect, or past continuous. In some cases both forms are possible.

It *be*[1] the first time that three friends *find*[2] a job. They *work*[3] on a building site, building a wall. After they had been there for a few hours the foreman *come*[4] to see them. He was surprised to find one of them already *build*[5] a complete wall, while the other two *stand*[6] doing nothing. They said they not *work*[7] because they were both lamp posts. The foreman *sack*[8] the two men immediately. As soon as his two friends had gone home, the man digging the hole also *stop*[9] work. 'It's OK,' said the foreman. 'I haven't sacked you. You *work*[10] very well, so carry on.' The man *reply*[11]: 'That's all very well saying I can keep my job, but how do you expect me to work in the dark?'

13 Present perfect

have / has + past participle

1 The present perfect often connects the past to the present. The action took place in the past but is not explicitly specified because we are more interested in the result than in the action itself.
*I'**ve bought** so many books that I don't know where to put them.*
*I can see that you'**ve made** a lot of progress.*

We use the present perfect for:
a actions that took place during a period that has not yet finished.
*The stock market **has crashed** twice this year. (It's only August.)*
b actions which took place at an indefinite or unknown time.
*I'**ve taken** part in three videoconferences.*

c actions that began in the past and continue into the present.
> I **have worked** for here six months.
> We'**ve made** a lot of progress in this project so far.

d to announce news.
> My email address **has changed**.
> We **have redesigned** our website.

e in emails and on the phone to indicate what actions have been taken.
> I **have spoken** to Invoice Processing and they **have forwarded** your request to the manager.

2 For and since are often used with the present perfect. When talking about an action's duration we use for if we talk about the period of time, and since if when say when the action began.
e.g. *for six years, for a long time, for more than an hour.*
since 2001, since January, since he joined the company.

Other time expressions typically associated with the present perfect are:
ever, never; just, already, yet; in the last few days / months etc., all day, all week, all my life etc., how long, once, twice, several times, etc.

Many of the above expressions can also be used with the past simple, if they refer to a completed period of time:

We'**ve made** a lot of money this first quarter. (Said in March – the first quarter of the year hasn't finished.)
We **made** a lot of money this first quarter. (Said in April or later – the first quarter is complete.)

3 The present perfect is used to talk about past events when no specific time is given.

However, if we go on to give more specific information about the subject and start talking about a specific date, we have to use the past simple.
*I'**ve bought** a lot of stuff from Amazon.* (not very specific information)
*What exactly **did** you buy? How long **did** it **take** to receive your orders?* (specifying)

A Complete the expressions with *for* or *since*, as appropriate.

1 _____ the company was founded
2 _____ more than a year
3 _____ the introduction of the euro
4 _____ the last six weeks
5 _____ she got her degree
6 _____ I've known you

B Put the verbs in italics in the news report into the present simple, present perfect, or past simple.

Devco *announced / have announced*[1] that they are going to buy their competitors QXT. QXT *is / has been*[2] in serious financial problems for over a year – last quarter's profits *were / have been*[3] down again by 60%. In a statement released earlier today Devco's CEO, Alfonso Fuego, *said / has said*[4]: 'We *had / have had*[5] a lot of support from QXT shareholders and I *assured / have assured*[6] them at the shareholders' meeting last week that Devco will do everything to turn the situation around within at most six months. QXT union members *are not / have not been*[7] so confident. In a meeting last Friday they *revealed / have revealed*[8] that they *are / have been worried*[9] about their jobs since news of a possible takeover *has been / was leaked*[10] to the press earlier this year.

C Match the beginnings with the correct endings.

1 She's been in Paris for six weeks …
  a she's learning French there.
  b she learnt French there.
2 They've gone to NY for a year …
  a they'll be back next Spring.
  b they came back last Spring.
3 She was his project leader for six months and he …
  a learnt a lot from her.
  b has learnt a lot.
4 I am here for six months …
  a it will be a great experience.
  b I have really enjoyed it.
5 I have been responsible for the Asian market …
  a among other markets.
  b and then after the African market.

14 Present perfect continuous

have / has + been + past participle

1 We use the present perfect continuous:
a to describe actions and trends that started in the past and continue in the present. We are interested in the process as well as the result.
> How long **have you been working** here?
> I'**ve been writing** the report all morning.

b to talk about the effect of recent events.
> Why are you covered in ink? I'**ve been repairing** the photocopier.

*He's **been working** for fourteen hours non-stop that's why he looks so tired.*

  c in emails and on the telephone to outline problems or to introduce a topic.
     *I gather you **have been experiencing** problems in ordering our products.*
     *I'**ve been talking** to Jim about the fault in your computer but I can't find your email describing …*

2 The present perfect continuous is not used:
  a for completed actions – compare:
     Interest rates have reached 8%. (a completed action)
     Interest rates have been going up all year. (and have not stopped going up)
  b To specifically quantify an action, e.g. talk about the number of times it happened. Use the present perfect simple instead – compare:
     He's been talking on the phone all morning. (and he is still talking now)
     He's made a least 25 phone calls this morning.

A Underline the correct form in italics.

  1 I have *written / been writing* emails all morning – I have *written / been writing* 20 so far.
  2 We have *received / been receiving* no reply to our request for information.
  3 He has *worked / been working* too hard that's why he's always so tired.
  4 He has *worked / been working* for several different companies. He has *worked / been working* for his current company for six months.
  5 They have *known / been knowing* each other since they were at school together.

B Read these extracts from emails and letters. Put the verbs in italics into the past simple, present perfect, or present perfect continuous.

  1 I hear you *have* problems with the new system. Sorry about this. I *speak* to the Systems Manager and she *promise* to get back to you by lunchtime. She also *ask* me if you could send her the log file.
  2 Thanks for buying me lunch yesterday. Great to see you. It made a nice change as I *be* so busy lately. By the way, I *forget* to ask you if you could give me your boss's email address. We *work* on a project recently which I think she would be interested in. Anyway take care and speak to you soon.

---

  3 We note from our records that we still not *receive* any payment for our invoice dated 3 March, reference number ZX45791. I would like to point out that this is the third time we *request* payment. I would be grateful if you would contact me about this as a matter of urgency. I *try* to ring you several times and I *leave* several messages with your secretary. I enclose a further copy of our invoice.

C For **1** and **2**, choose the correct answer. For **3** and **4**, say which part in italics is not correct and why.

  1 *She's been living here for six months.* When did she arrive?
     a six months ago   **b** we don't know
  2 *I've been reading a computer manual.* Does this mean that I have completed the manual?
     a yes   **b** probably not
  3 I've been having *problems / a car* since June.
  4 He has been smoking *all morning / 50 cigarettes this morning.*

15 Present simple

I work → he works   **you catch → she catches**
we try → she tries   **you go → she goes**

1 We use the present simple:
  a to describe states and situations that are permanent and always true.
     *The President **lives** in the White House.*
     *The earth **revolves** around the sun.*
  b to talk about habits and things that we do regularly.
     *I **work** for an Internet service provider.*
     *She **leaves** home at 6.30 every morning.*
  c in formal emails and letters to say why we are writing, what we are attaching, etc.
     *I **write** to complain about the poor service …*
     *I **enclose** the budget estimates you requested.*
     *I **look** forward to hearing from you in the near future.*

Time expressions typically associated with the present simple are: *frequently, often, occasionally, etc. every day, on Saturdays, each week, once a year.*

2 The present simple is not used:

a to make suggestions, ask for advice, or offer to do things. Use *shall* or *will* instead.
Shall *we go out for dinner tonight?*
Shall *I ring you to confirm the arrangements?*
I **will** *let you know the results of the tests tomorrow.*

b for actions or situations that began in the past and continue into the present. Use the present perfect instead.
I **have lived** *here for six months. (Not: I live here for six months.)*

16 Present continuous

be (am / is / are) + verb + ing

1 We use the present continuous:

a to describe an incomplete action that is going on, now at this moment.
You **are reading** *an explanation of the present continuous.*
The sun **is shining** *outside.*

b to talk about an incomplete action that is going on now, in this present period. Here *now* has a wider sense than *now, this moment*.
We're **working** *on a new project.*
The number of people using the Internet **is growing** *constantly.*

c to talk about a temporary event or situation.
I usually work in my own office, but today I'm **working** *in Carol's office.*
She's **staying** *in a hotel until she finds a flat to rent.*

d in emails and letters to give a less formal and more friendly tone, particularly with verbs such as *write, enclose, attach, look forward to.*
I **am attaching** *those photos of the kids I told you about.*
I'm really **looking forward** *to seeing you again.*

e to talk about future arrangements (see *future*).

Time expressions typically associated with the present continuous are: *currently, now, at the moment, for a few weeks, in this period, this week, next month.*

2 Some verbs are never used in the continuous form. The majority of these are verbs that describe a state rather than an action.

a verbs which describe an opinion or mental state: *believe, forget, imagine, know, mean, notice, recognize, remember, think* (i.e. have an opinion, not the activity), *understand.*
I **understand** *you have had some problems with the new machine.*

b auxiliaries and modals: *be, have, can, must, should.*
There **is** *a meeting on Friday,* **can** *you come?*

c senses and perception: *feel, hear, see, seem, look, smell, taste.*
This room **smells** *of gas.*

d emotions and desires: e.g. *hate, hope, like, love, prefer, regret, want, wish.*
We **regret** *to inform you that …*

e measurement: e.g. *contain, cost, hold, measure, weigh.*
This package **contains** *the start-up software.*

3 In cases where these verbs are used to refer to actions rather than states, they may be used in the continuous form.
We **are having** *dinner with the president on Friday.* (have means 'eat' not 'possess')
We **were thinking** *about opening a new office.* (think means 'consider' not 'have an opinion')

A Put the verbs in italics into the correct tense.

1 It's *raining / rains* very hard. Can you give me a lift home?
2 I *don't have / am not having* much spare time at the moment. I'm *studying / study* to pass an exam.
3 The price of shares *varies / is varying* according to economic conditions.
4 I *speak / am speaking* French fluently because I grew up in Paris, but I'm *forgetting / forget* my German because I never use it.
5 Anne normally *deals / is dealing* with enquiries from overseas, but I'm *dealing / deal* with this one.

B In each of the following sentences, put one of the verbs into the present simple and one into the present continuous.

1 What he (talk) about? I (not understand)!
2 I'm afraid Mr Passos is (have) lunch at the moment. (Have) an appointment?
3 We (interview) candidates for a new managerial post at the moment, but we urgently (need) more secretarial staff.
4 The new model (perform) very well in all weather conditions. It's not surprising that it (become) more and more popular.
5 I (think about) applying for the post in the Accounts Department. It (depend) what the salary is.

17 Useful language for emails

1 Beginnings and endings

Dear James
Dear James Bond
Dear Mr Bond (formal) (NB Mr – male, Ms – female)
Hi! (informal)
Speak to you soon. (informal)
I look forward to hearing from you.
I am looking forward to hearing from you.
    (informal)
Kind / Best regards / wishes
All the best, (informal)
Yours sincerely / faithfully (very formal)

2 Giving main reason for message

Just to let you know that …
This email is intended to inform you that …
(formal)
I am writing to you because …
Your address was given to me by …

3 Making and replying to inquiries

I would like to know …
Could you possibly send me …
Any information you could give us would be
    appreciated.
Thanks in advance.
With reference to / … Re / Regarding your inquiry …
Further to our conversation of yesterday,
As requested I am sending you …
Please note that …
We would like to point out that …
Please feel free to contact me if you have any
    questions.

4 Referring to the next step in the proceedings

Please have a look at the enclosed report and let
me know what you think.
Re your request. I'll look into it and send you a
reply by the end of the week.
I will contact you when I return.
Do you want / Would you like me to …
Shall I …?
Let me know whether …
Please could you get back to me by the end of
today / this morning / asap.

5 Sending, receiving, and chasing emails and attachments

Please find attached …
Please confirm / acknowledge receipt.
I confirm receipt of your email.

I received / got your email, but I'm afraid I can't
    open the attachment.
Thanks for your email but I'm afraid you forgot to
    send the attachment.
Did you get my last message sent on …?
May we remind you that we are still awaiting your
    reply to our message dated … (formal)

6 Arrangements

Can we arrange a meeting on …
Will try and call you Monday to confirm.
Would love to meet – but not this week! I can
    manage Nov 16 or 17th if either of those suit.
    (informal)
Sorry, can't make the meeting at 13.00. Could we
    change it to14.00? (informal)
Re our meeting next week. I am afraid something
    has come up and I need to change the time.
    Would it be possible on Tuesday 13 at 15.00?
    (neutral)
We were due to meet next Tuesday afternoon. Is
    there any chance I could move it until later in
    the week? Wed or Thur perhaps? Please let me
    know your availability. (formal)
I look forward to seeing you on 30 November.
OK, Wednesday, March 10 at 11.00. I look forward
    to seeing you then.

7 Thanking and apologizing

Many thanks for your email.
Thanks for getting back to me.
Thank you for the quick response.
Cheers. (informal)
Sorry for the delay in getting back to you / replying
… but I have been out of the office.
… but I've been away this week / for the last few
    days.

8 Asking for and giving clarification

I'm not sure what you mean by …
What exactly do you mean by …?
Sorry, what's a 'xxx'?
What I meant by x is …
I'm assuming you mean …
Do you mean that …?
I hope this helps clarify the problems.

9 Out of office message

… is on leave from Monday 07/08 to Wed 16/08. If
you have any problems or queries please contact
the IT office on extention 1234.

18 Useful language for making arrangements

Inviting

Would you like to have lunch?
Do you fancy lunch?
How about / what about going to theatre this evening?

Accepting an offer

I'd be delighted.
Sure I'd love to.
I'd really like that.

Suggesting a day / time

Would next Tuesday suit you?
How about next Tuesday?
How about / what about Saturday afternoon?

Declining a day / time and suggesting alternatives

No, I'm sorry I can't make Tuesday.
I'm sorry Tuesday's not possible.

I'm afraid I've got something else on on Saturday.
What about Friday then?
Would Friday be more convenient for you?

Changing

Could we move it to …?
Would you mind if we changed it to …?

Apologizing and accepting apologies

I'm sorry I can't because … (give reason).
I'm really sorry about that.
No problem.
Don't worry, that's quite alright.

Checking

Let me just check my diary.
Hang on while I check.

Ending a conversation

I look forward to seeing you.
Take care and bye for now.

19 Useful language for meetings

1 Starting a meeting

I'd like to start the meeting by …
Let's begin by looking at the first item on the agenda.
OK shall we start?

2 Asking for opinions

Does anyone have any comments / anything to say about this?
What do you think about …?

3 Giving opinions

I think we need to …
What about if we …

4 Moving on

Let's look at the next item on the agenda.
We need to move on to the next point.

5 Keeping to the agenda

Thanks, that's a good point. Shall we put it on the agenda for the next meeting?
We can discuss that in more detail later on / at the next meeting.
To continue, the next item on this agenda is …

6 Interrupting

Sorry – can I just say …
I would just like to add that …

7 Handling interruptions

Pete – you were saying?
Can I just finish what I was saying?

8 Ending a meeting

I think we've covered everything so let's finish here.
This is a good point to end the meeting.

1 Receiving calls

How can I help you?
Can I ask the name of your company?
Can you repeat the name of your company?
Who shall I say is calling?
Sorry, who did you say you wanted to speak to?
Sorry, where are you calling from?

2 If you can't understand

Could you repeat that please?
Sorry, what was that?
I'm sorry but the line's bad (I can hardly hear you.)
Could you speak up a little, please?
Could you speak a little more slowly please?
I'm so sorry we got cut off.

3 Putting someone through

I'll see if I can put you through.
Hold the line please. I'll see if she's back from lunch.
I'll put you on hold.
Just a moment … ringing for you.
Sorry to keep you waiting Mr Thomas,
I can put you through to Mr Dameri now.

4 Person called is not available

I'm afraid you've just missed him –
   he should be back in about half an hour.
I'm sorry but he's not in his office.
I'm afraid he's away on holiday.
He'll be back at the beginning of next week.
He's in a meeting.
Hello, the line's engaged, can you hold or would
   you like to call back later?
Thank you for calling, goodbye.

5 Taking a message

Can I take a message?
Would you like to leave a message?
Can you spell that please?
Can I read that back to you?
So the number is 0207 999 6766?
So that's …
OK, no problem. I'll leave that for him.

6 Leaving a message

This is Carl Jones calling from Kandart in Sydney.
   Could I leave a message for Hillary Leon please?

Could you ask her to ring me back on 02 878 705
   (oh two / eight seven eight / seven oh five).
I'm sorry but I gave you the wrong number. It's
   two one six, not two three six.
That's seventeen – one seven.
No, that's Rosi with an 'i' not an 'a'.
I'll spell that again for you.
Yes, that's right.
Thanks for your help.

7 Phoning another company

Good morning, this is Lee Sellars from Kandart
   Sydney.
Could you put me through to Mr Thomas / the
   Personnel Department?
I would like to speak to Mr Smith from
   Administration.
Could you give me extension 215 please?
I'd like to speak to someone about …

8 Person not available

Can you tell me when he'll be back?
Can I leave a message?
Right, I'll call again next week.
Could he possibly call me back? My name's
Mr Dameri and my number is …
Could he possibly call me as soon as he comes back
   as it's rather urgent?

9 Arranging a meeting for third parties

I would like to arrange a meeting between Mr R and
   Mr S.
Is Mr S free in the morning of Wednesday the 6th in
   his office?
Could you send me an email to confirm whether
   this is possible.
If the 6th is no good, can you suggest a better day?
The 8th is better for us.

10 Changing arrangements for third parties

I'm awfully sorry, but Mr R won't be able to make
   the meeting on the 6th.
Could we possible change it and make it the 7th
   instead?
Could you check with Mr S and ring me back?
Thanks very much for your help and please send
   my apologies to Mr S.

21 Useful language for presentations

1 Introducing

Let me start by giving you a brief outline of my talk.
Firstly I'll examine …
Then we'll take a look at …
Finally, I'll outline … If anyone has any questions, please save them for the end.
Please feel free to stop me if you have any questions.

2 Visual aids

As you can see from the chart …
If you take a look at this graph …

3 Moving on

Now let's move on to …
The next issue is to look at …

4 Summarizing

So we've looked at …
I'd like to sum up the main points again.
I'd just like to go over …

5 Concluding

So what does all this mean?
To conclude I would like to stress that …

6 Closing

That's brings me to the end of my talk.
Thanks you for being such a good audience.
Does anyone have any questions?

22 Verb list

Infinitive	Past tense	Past participle
be	was / were	been
become	became	become
begin	began	begun
bite	bit	bitten
blow	blew	blown
break	broke	broken
bring	brought	brought
build	built	built
burn	burnt	burnt
buy	bought	bought
catch	caught	caught
choose	chose	chosen
come	came	come
cost	cost	cost
cut	cut	cut
do	did	done
draw	drew	drawn
drink	drank	drunk
drive	drove	driven
eat	ate	eaten
fall	fell	fallen
feed	fed	fed
feel	felt	felt
fight	fought	fought
find	found	found
fly	flew	flown
forget	forgot	forgotten
freeze	froze	frozen
get	got	got
give	gave	given
go	went	been / gone

Infinitive	Past tense	Past participle
grow	grew	grown
hang	hung	hung
have	had	had
hear	heard	heard
hide	hid	hidden
hit	hit	hit
hold	held	held
hurt	hurt	hurt
keep	kept	kept
know	knew	known
lead	led	led
learn	learnt	learnt
leave	left	left
lend	lent	lent
let	let	let
lose	lost	lost
make	made	made
mean	meant	meant
meet	met	met
pay	paid	paid
put	put	put
read	read	read
ride	rode	ridden
ring	rang	rung
rise	rose	risen
run	ran	run
say	said	said
see	saw	seen
sell	sold	sold
send	sent	sent
set	set	set
shake	shook	shaken
shine	shone	shone
shoot	shot	shot
show	showed	shown
shut	shut	shut
sing	sang	sung
sink	sank	sunk
sleep	slept	slept
speak	spoke	spoken
spend	spent	spent
spread	spread	spread
stand	stood	stood
steal	stole	stolen
stick	stuck	stuck
strike	struck	struck
swim	swam	swum
take	took	taken
teach	taught	taught
tear	tore	torn
tell	told	told
think	thought	thought
throw	threw	thrown
wake	woke	woken
wear	wore	worn
win	won	won
write	wrote	written

1A

1 faster   fastest
2 cheaper   cheapest
3 fatter   fattest
4 later   latest
5 better   best
6 worse   worst
7 further   furthest
8 happier   happiest
9 more feasible   most feasible

1B

1 than
2 more
3 biggest
4 the least
5 younger
6 most
7 more
8 more
9 likely
10 than
11 as
12 as
13 more
14 than
15 as

2A

1 e   3 f   5 d
2 c   4 a   6 b

2B

1 press, will
2 will, see
3 were, would
4 would, had
5 would, won

2C

1 asked
2 would probably get
3 asked
4 would be
5 could

3A

1 U   4 U   7 U   10 C
2 U   5 C   8 U   11 U
3 C   6 U   9 C   12 U

3B

1 some
2 each or every
3 every
4 every
5 several

(4)

6 many
7 all
8 any
9 enough
10 little

4A

1 are preparing
2 will have
3 will stay
4 are launching or are going to launch
5 will probably start
6 will beat
7 are going to send
8 are you going to do
9 will melt
10 won't
11 are going to send

4B

1 will fetch him
2 am going on holiday
3 are going ahead in May
4 will order some more
5 will call the engineer
6 is going to take / is taking a job in New York

4C

1 are selling
2 am meeting
3 will help
4 are going to
5 is teaching

5A

1 to study
2 posing
3 repeating
4 to connect
5 to gain
6 writing

5B

1 to continue
2 showing
3 encouraging
4 working
5 to leave
6 cutting
7 watching

6A

1 on the other hand
2 in fact
3 also
4 moreover
5 however

6B

1 consequently
2 moreover
3 also
4 however
5 although
6 finally

7.1 A

1 may
2 could
3 will
4 could

7.1 B

students' own answers

7.2 A

1 don't have to
2 mustn't
3 have to
4 must
5 should

7.2 B

students' own answers

7.3

possible answers:
1 Could I send a fax please?
2 Could you phone for a taxi for me please?
3 Would you mind if I smoke/smoked?
4 Could you explain this to me please?
5 Would you like to come for dinner?
6 Can I help you with your luggage?
7 Shall we have a break?
8 Could you bring me the bill please?
9 Could you help me with my luggage please?
10 Could you tell me when breakfast is served?

8

Possible answers:
1 When did you start your current job?
2 How much did you weigh when you were 18?
3 What for you is the ideal temperature on a summer's day?
4 How much per square metre does a flat in your town cost?
5 What percentage of your day do you spend on the phone?
6 What is your home phone number?
7 Could you give me Anna's email address?

8 What do you think the ratio of work to leisure should be?

9 What for you is the ideal length of a business lunch?

9A

1 were sold
2 has been promoted
3 have promoted
4 was decided, should be discontinued
5 has
6 has
7 has
8 was
9 was
10 had been lost

9B

1 occurred
2 noticed
3 was brought
4 were taken
5 was fumigated
6 was checked
7 was suspected
8 decided
9 came
10 unplugged

9C

1 I have forwarded your email to the Marketing Department.
2 Please complete the form in black ink.
3 We carried out an analysis. / We analysed the samples.
4 Remember the following points when dealing with complaints.

11A

1 was sleeping, went
2 did you do
3 did
4 lived, moved

11B

1 used
2 left
3 was telling
4 did

12A

1 had seen, didn't want
2 left
3 explained, had finished
4 thought, had told

12B

1 had worked
2 was
3 had come
4 left

12C

1 was
2 had found
3 were working
4 came
5 had already built
6 were standing
7 were not working
8 sacked
9 stopped
10 were working
11 replied

13A

1 since
2 for
3 since
4 for
5 since
6 since

13B

1 have announced
2 has been
3 were
4 said
5 have had
6 assured
7 are not
8 revealed
9 have been worried
10 was leaked

13C

1 a   **2** a   **3** a   **4** a   **5** a

14A

1 been writing, written
2 received
3 been working
4 worked / been working
5 known

14B

1 have had / have been having, spoke / have spoken, promised, asked
2 have been, forgot, have been working
3 have still not received, have requested, have tried, have left

14C

1 a
2 b
3 a car is not correct because when have means to possess we don't use the continuous form. On the other hand, we have been having problems is correct because in this case have means to experience rather than to possess.

4 50 cigarettes this morning is not correct because when we have a quantity (which is not a time quantity) then we don't use the continuous form, otherwise it would mean that he had 50 cigarettes in his mouth at the same time!

16A

1 It's raining
2 I don't have / I'm studying
3 varies
4 I speak / I'm forgetting
5 deals / I'm dealing

16B

1 is he talking / don't understand
2 is having / do you have
3 are interviewing / need
4 performs / is becoming
5 thinking about / depends

Unit 1

(((1.1)))

1 A: I'm the promotions manager here in New York for a multinational recording company based in Tokyo. We have a turnover of about 60 billion dollars a year.

B: Wow! sounds interesting. How many people work there?

A: In Tokyo only about 2,000, but in the offices around the world, probably another 10,000.

B: That's a lot of people. So do you live here in New York?

A: For the moment yes but it's only temporary. I'm working here for the moment, but last year I was in Bonn, and next year I'll be in Rome.

B: You're the Promotions Manager, so who's your boss?

A: I report to the Marketing Manager.

B: And what does your job involve?

A: Well our core business is music CDs, so basically I'm responsible for promoting the key new groups, for ensuring that they get seen and heard as much as possible.

B: Sounds fun.

A: Yeah but more often than not I work very long hours. At the moment for example, I'm going to lots of late night concerts which you get sick of after a while.

B: Yeah, I suppose if you're doing it all the time. But do you meet some interesting people?

A: Yeah, I meet all the groups and travel to some exciting places but you know pop stars can be very demanding – they don't turn up for interviews and scheduling anything is a nightmare; and often I don't always like their music.

B: No, sure.

A: At the moment I'm promoting a group of 16-year-olds who really need a mother to look after them more than a manager.

2 A: Well I'm an senior partner in a firm of accountants in Paris. There are about 50 employees and I am directly responsible to the shareholders.

B: And tell me, what's that like? I mean is being an accountant really as boring as it sounds?

A: To be honest with you, I really enjoy it. There is something very satisfying about doing essential work for clients which you know they find rather difficult and tedious.

B: So you mean you know that your clients appreciate what you do?

A: Exactly. Clients mostly ring me for help and advice and it's great when you can find ways of saving people money.

B: By avoiding taxes you mean?

A: Well it is fun if it's legal, of course! And it's interesting finding out about other people's work which varies a lot. I'm responsible for clients in various fashion houses in Paris.

B: And is it stressful work?

A: Well it can be, you know. I'm learning new things all the time as tax policies change so much. At the moment I'm focusing on some changes that have just been introduced by the European Parliament, so that means I have to …

(((1.2)))

A: Can you tell me a bit about how employees have a voice within the company?

B: Well each year we elect six people to be the barometer really for the company, for how people are feeling in the company, for non-business, non-commercial decisions.

A: And what about the office environment, how important is that? Because obviously looking around me here it is quite a different, different place to work.

B: Well um the most important element in this office is in the sense that there is no office. You can see we've got er no desks; I've got no personal space in this building other than a small metal locker which is totally inadequate for my large amounts of rubbish that I collect.

A: And that's the same for everybody then, everyone has just a locker?

B: Yeah that's the same for everybody.

A: No one has a desk?

B: No, no one has a desk. No one has anything but a little locker.

A: And how do you know then where you going to be when you come in to work in the morning?

B: Well er when you come into work um you grab a small, well we have some special phones designed by Ericsson for us, which mean that you can walk around the building with them, so you have your own personal line. They are wireless; you walk around the building and you just choose where you want to work [Right]. We're sitting here in one of our brand rooms and the brand rooms are the only er proprietorial spaces in the building. That's to say that each client has its own brand room, so opposite us you've got the HSBC er bank. Downstairs you'll find the Clark shoes room, the um Travelocity room, er the IPC room. Next door we've got the IKEA room.

B: And what that creates again is, is an atmosphere of trust, you know this is not about having your own little office with your secretary outside and you know, all your own copies of everything.

A: So there is a free flow of information within the company?

B: Completely free flow of information.

A: Of all information?

B: Of all information. Of all information, of financial information. The only um information that we um don't have kind of freely available is salaries, although you can go and ask to know people's salary.

A: And what about perks? Are there any other company perks that …?

B: I think the greatest perk is, I mean, let me tell you the perks are yes, very good healthcare, you know gym membership, um er the 'make yourself more interesting fund' which we all get every year to do go off and do whatever you want to do with.

A: Wow that sounds good.

B: Yeah, well people do all sorts of things from yoga to abseiling to, you know, to massage too. We have yoga here. We have tai chi. We have very very good subsidized organic food downstairs every day.

A: What about working hours, does the company encourage long working hours, generally speaking?
B: I don't think, I don't think we work particularly long hours, I think we work healthy hours. I think we work when we know we need to work. Um so I, you know, I have flexibility to get out, you know, I go to the gym most lunchtimes. Um so that's whatever, an hour and a half but then I probably stay till 7.30; quite often I'll do a little bit of work at home in the evenings. I don't think it's particularly long hours.

(((1.4)))

Example: E C G P S
1 A H J K R   4 O H R
2 E B D J T X   5 U V Q W
3 I C P Y Z   6 F E L M N S X

(((1.5)))

1 C: Hi, this is Sara. I'm just ringing to give you Courtney's email address.
   D: Oh great, thanks.
   C: It's Courtney Fir, that's c-o-u-r-t-n-e-y dot fir, f-i-r at isnet.co.fr.
   D: Isnet? i-z-n-e-t?
   C: No i-S-n-e-t dot co dot fr. And his mobile is 0033 897 6546 987.

2 E: My address is yasmin.del_corso at hotmail dot com. y-a-s-m-i-n dot d-e-l underscore c-o-r-s-o at hotmail dot com.
   F: Sorry I didn't understand what comes after yasmin.
   E: Underscore, the little line, like a hyphen.
   F: OK I'm with you. So it's y-a-s-m-i-n dot d-e-l underscore c-o-r-s-o at hotmail dot com. All lower case right?
   E: Yep. And you can phone me on 001 897 664 3215.

3 A: Could you ask him to email me the pricelist. It's Shelagh Baines, no dots, at Meta dot uk. All lower case. That's Shelagh S-H-E-L-A-G-H Baines B-A-I-N-E-S at Meta M-E-T-A dot uk, shelaghbaines@meta.uk. Have you got that?
   B: Yes. I think he also wanted the website, the one with the project reviews, do you happen to know it?
   A: Yes he did, you're right. Well it's www dot meta dot co dot uk forward slash projects underscore two three four.
   B: I'll just read that back: www dot meta dot co dot uk forward slash projects underscore two three four.
   A: Brilliant. Thanks.

(((1.6)))

1 A: This is Oscar Mendes.
2 B: Could I speak to Paolo Rossi please?
3 A: Could I leave a message?
4 B: Who's calling please?
5 A: Can I help you?
6 B: Could you spell that for me?

(((1.7)))

1 A: Could I speak to Paolo Rossi please?
   B: Speaking.
   A: This is Oscar Mendes from Panac. I was given your

name by Tim Hucks, who told me you were responsible for marketing the JTC software.
   B: Actually I'm no longer in the JTC department. I'll just put you through to Tonia Burova who's taken over from me. Could you hold on a moment, please? (pause) Sorry, Tonia's in a meeting at the moment.
   A: Could I leave a message?
   B: Yes of course.
   A: Could you ask her to call me on 0206 7677 987?
   B: 0206 7677 987 and could I have your name again please?
   A: Oscar Mendes.
   B: Could you spell that for me?
   A: O-s-c-a-r new word M-e-n-d-e-s.
   B: OK Oscar, I'll get Tonia to ring you as soon as possible.
   A: Thanks a lot. Bye.

2 A: Quantex, good morning, Monica speaking. Can I help you?
   B: Could I speak to Carlos Santana please?
   A: Can I ask who's calling please?
   B: Brad Caroli.
   A: One moment please. Sorry his line's engaged. Would you like to leave a message?
   B: Yes could you tell him that Brad Caroli called that's b-r-a-d new word c-a-r-o-l-i, and the meeting's been rescheduled for next Tuesday, that's Tuesday the thirteenth.
   A: Tuesday the thirteenth.
   B: Yes, and if there are any problems he can get me on my cell phone. The number is 0338 301 4467.
   A: 0338 301 44 ...?
   B: 4467.
   A: 4467, OK. I'll make sure he gets your message.

Unit 2

(((2.1)))

A: When was the first Ferrari car made?
B: The first Ferrari carrying the Ferrari badge was made in 1947 which was a Ferrari 125S. Enzo Ferrari when he created the company in about 1939 was still under licence to Alfa Romeo, because he ran the Alfa Romeo racing car team. But he came here to Maranello and built his first car but without the Ferrari name on it in 1945. So there was a car before although it was made by Ferrari er which technically is not a Ferrari. Sounds complicated but the first car to bear the Ferrari name was in 1947.
A: OK and does that car still exist?
B: That particular car, I don't think exists anymore. It won the Grand Prix of Rome that year and I think under the policy of Enzo Ferrari, which was to sell each car after it had done a race to finance the next car. It may exist in parts somewhere in terms of the engine or the gear box but as a whole I don't think it exists anymore.
A: OK. Was it red?
B: Yes it was red. Every car at that particular time ran under the national racing colours: France was blue; America was white; England was green. And er Italy was red [represented Italy] and so so that's why the car was red.
A: OK and when did Ferrari stop producing exclusively red cars?
B: Well Ferrari's always offered the option to customers to have the car whatever colour they want. So we've had green Ferraris. We've had blue Ferraris but predominantly people have wanted them in red because they associate red with Ferrari.

A: Can you tell me a bit about your job? What's your role in Ferrari?

B: Well like most jobs within Ferrari, the my role here is, is, covers a multitude of things from looking after the press, to dealing with Formula One, to dealing with road cars, launching cars, working with clients, talking with the press, working with the press, motor shows. It covers a whole breadth of things. We're such a small company. We're 2,000 people in total and that 2,000 people are designing cars, making cars. We make everything here. My job is to really sort of present the image of Ferrari, to check that the image is being correctly presented with the press, to be accessible to the press. Er for example when Michael Schumacher broke his leg at Silverstone a year ago I happened to be at Silverstone at the time and I was responsible for the press conferences and the press liaison between Ferrari and the international media. Um because we're always in the spotlight, because Ferrari is always making news, er you tend to find that every single day that we've got either TV or journalists or magazines wanting to come to the factory to interview people, to test the cars. It's very difficult; it's not an easy job to do.

A: So it's quite a varied job but for you what's the most interesting aspect?

B: I think the most interesting aspect for me is the pace of change here at Ferrari. Things happen extremely quickly. Because we're small, we can agree to do something and we can do it very quickly and execute it very quickly. And I think also the the excitement of Ferrari and I still think you know the day that a Ferrari, you get behind the wheel of a Ferrari, and it doesn't excite you is probably the day to pack up and leave Maranello.

A: And how long have you been working for the company?

B: In total I've worked for Ferrari for seven years. Four years in the UK as Sales and Marketing Director and three years now here in Italy. So er great experience but even more I think for an Englishman to be in, in very much an Italian company.

(((2.3)))

offered, worked, created

(((2.4)))

offered:	happened, followed, moved, joined, remembered
worked:	launched, watched, experienced, stressed, developed
created:	restricted, studied

(((2.5)))

1 business   2 secondary   3 different

(((2.6)))

1	secretary	5	comfortable
2	interesting	6	temperature
3	Wednesday	7	personal
4	preferable	8	average

(((2.7)))

A: Hi, you must be our new Marketing Manager.

B: Yes that's right.

A: I'm Mika Yoshimoto. I'm in the Sales Department. (long pause) And you're here for the meeting?

B: Uh huh.

A: I thought I was going to be late. The traffic was awful, wasn't it?

B: Yes it was.

A: Have you seen the agenda for the meeting?

B: Yes, I have.

A: I haven't. Are there a lot of points to cover?

B: About ten I think.

A: I suppose we'll be talking about our new trading partners.

B: Probably yes.

A: I hate these long meetings, don't you?

B: Yes.

A: So how's the new job going? You've been here about a week now I suppose.

B: Yes, that's right.

A: Do you fancy a quick cup of coffee before the meeting starts and then you can tell me all about it?

B: No, I've just had one.

(((2.8)))

A: Hi, you must be our new Marketing Manager.

B: Yes that's right. Pedro Diaz, pleased to meet you.

A: Mika Yoshimoto, I'm in Sales.

B: In Sales?

A: Yes that's right. And you're here for the meeting?

B: Yeah, actually I thought I was going to be late. The traffic was awful, wasn't it?

A: Actually I came here by train.

B: Oh did you? And have you seen the agenda for the meeting?

A: Yes, it looks like we've got a lot of points to cover.

B: I suppose we'll be talking about our new trading partners.

A: Yeah I should imagine so, but I hate these long meetings, don't you?

B: Generally speaking, but I think this one will give me an opportunity to meet the team.

A: Right of course. So how's the new job going? You've been here about a week now I suppose.

B: Yes, that's right. It's going fine. What about you, how long have you been here?

A: About five years now.

B: Five years, really?

(((2.9)))

A: Did you watch any TV last night?

B: No actually I didn't – why was there anything good on?

A: Well there was this travel programme about Australia. It showed these amazing trips you can go into the desert – sleeping under the stars. It was incredible.

B: Wow sounds amazing. You know I've been to Australia once, but not to the desert.

A: Really? So where did you go?

B: To Sydney and up to Queensland then to the coral reef.

A: That must be interesting too. Did you go diving?

B: No, I didn't have the time but we did do some snorkelling.

A: And did you like Sydney?

B: Yes, it's a very attractive city. But you know when I was there it rained every day.

A: Every day? Is that unusual.

B: Well apparently Sydney does get a lot of rain but I think I was a bit unlucky. So are you thinking of going to Australia?

Unit 3

A: OK how long have you been working in the field of business training videos?

B: Er as a business Video Arts was started in 1972, so we've been operating for very nearly 30 years, now.

A: Wow, a long time! [That started, sure.]

B: That that started actually producing 16 mm films [Right], when that was the er technology of the time. That's progressed through video and the video revolution and more latterly moved on to CD Rom and now online delivery of, of training products too.

A: What about the teaching of presentation skills, has that changed over the years?

B: It probably has done. One of the first Video Arts programmes was er er a video programme called *Making your case*, which looked at the skills of of giving a presentation. Now, some of those skills haven't changed at all in terms of, of good preparation and of knowing your audience [Right] What has probably changed more is the support that you have around your presentation which in the past may have just been chalk and talk er or a slide show at best, but now with the advent of technology and er Powerpoint and other er technologies, your presentation can become er something that's very spectacular very easily. [Yeah. OK].

A: Do you sell your videos to non-English-speaking countries?

B: We do. Video Arts is a worldwide phenomenon in terms of the products which are translated across all European languages. Erm it's possible to learn time management in Cantonese from John Cleese in actual fact, so it's certainly a worldwide message.

A: Right. And have you made any videos teaching native English speakers to communicate successfully with foreign partners?

B: In the past we have. Many years ago Video Arts produced a programme directed at doing business er overseas for UK business people [Right] erm. More recently er through a sister company we've produced a programme on building a transnational team which probably reflects that er most teams now have a global feel to them [Multicultural yeah]. May not meet but may be based in different countries and therefore actually understanding each other's cultures erm in whatever sphere of work is er an important part of the mix.

(((3.2)))

1 At **this** stage, I don't believe that we would be interested in your full range of services.

2 At this stage, I don't believe that we would be interested in your **full** range of services.

3 At this stage, I don't believe that **we** would be interested in your full range of services.

4 At this stage, I don't believe that we would be interested in your full range of services.

(((3.3)))

1 So I'm going to begin with a general history and background to the company. Then I'll go on to examine the take-over proposal in detail and what this could mean for you. Next I'll explore our possible alternative options and finally my recommendations. There should be enough time at the end for us to have a discussion and for you to ask any questions.

2 So I'm going to begin with a general history and background to the company. Then I'll go on to examine the take-over proposal in detail and what this could mean for you. Next I'll explore our possible alternative options and finally my recommendations. There should be enough time at the end for us to have a discussion and for you to ask any questions.

3 So I'm going to begin with a general history and background to the company. Then I'll go on to examine the take-over proposal in detail and what this could mean for you. Next I'll explore our possible alternative options and finally my recommendations. There should be enough time at the end for us to have a discussion and for you to ask any questions.

(((3.4)))

A: Can you give us any quick tips for making successful presentations?

B: Um, as I say the main areas where er presentations, er, either succeed or fail haven't changed in, in the 30 years that Video Arts have been covering them and those are really to … to first of all identify and prioritize the the key points that you want to communicate to your audience. [Right]. To actually prepare, which is something that we find for a lot of training areas, to actually looking at, erm, your support material or audiovisual aids and making sure that they make your presentation high impact. [Right]. The next thing is to actually conduct effective rehearsals. So don't go in cold and actually adapt er adapt a positive approach [yep] because if you think you're going to fail, then sure enough you [probably will] probably will. [Yes]. And the last thing is really just a tip for all presentations and that's to try and start strongly to engage people, er, to finish memorably with a …with a strong point and try and stay in control if you are er interacting with your audience at any time as well. [OK, thank you].

(((3.5)))

a I'm going to talk for about 30 minutes about how we can boost your sales figures with a new up-to-date dynamic ad campaign.

b In the first part of my talk, I will focus on the trends in TV advertising over the last five years. I will then examine why some of these ads have been more successful than others and how this relates to you. Finally I will present our recommendations. If you have any questions, please save them for the end when I'll be happy to discuss our ideas with you.

c Well that brings me to the end of my talk. Thank you very much for listening. Now does anyone have any questions?

d Good morning. I'd like to begin by introducing myself. My name is Tim Jackson and I'm the Creative Director of St Matthew's Advertising Agency.

e As you can see from my slide the least persuasive types of ads last year were those that used Company Directors or famous people to endorse products. This leads me to the most important part of my talk, our recommendations and the kind of advertising campaign we think will bring you significant results.

f So let's go over the most important points I would like you to remember from my talk today. For an effective ad campaign you need to be original and to entertain…

8 A: Yeah I've decided that I'm going to try and get that promotion.

B: Oh great.

1 A: Hello, could I speak to Serge Bertel please?

B: Speaking.

A: Oh hello it's Lulu Stader here. Sorry I didn't recognize your voice.

B: That's OK. What can I do for you?

A: Well it's about your proposal. Would you like to have lunch sometime next week, so we can discuss it further in a more relaxed environment?

B: That's an excellent idea; I'd be delighted. What day are you thinking of?

A: Well would next Tuesday suit you?

B: I'm sorry Tuesday's not possible. I'm going to Tripoli.

A: OK. Would next Friday be more convenient?

B: It should be OK but I'll ring you back to confirm.

A: Sure, no problem. I thought we could go to Adriano's restaurant but we can finalize the details later on in the week.

B: Sounds good. I'll ring you back as soon as I can.

A: OK, bye for now.

2 B: Hello. I said I'd get back to you about our lunch appointment.

A: Ah yes, is Friday still convenient for you?

B: Well actually no, I'm giving a presentation in the morning and it's quite likely to run on into lunch time. Could we move it to the following week, say Tuesday or Thursday? I'm really sorry about this but it's a very busy period for us.

A: Don't worry; that's quite all right. Let me just check my diary. OK Thursday the 13th would be better for me.

B: Good that suits me too.

A: OK. Shall we meet at Adriano's at say 1.00 p.m.?

B: Yes that's fine.

A: See you on the 13th then at 1.00 p.m.

A: Great. I look forward to seeing you.

A: This is a nice place; have you been here before?

B: Oh yes, our company uses it a lot. The food is reliably good and the service is usually pretty fast.

A: That's so important when you have to go back to work afterwards.

B: Exactly. So, have you decided what you're going to have? Do you need any help with the menu?

A: Yes thanks, just one thing. What exactly is hotpot?

B: Ah well it's a typical local dish, a bit like a meat and potato stew. I recommend it. It's really good,

A: OK I'll have that then. And just some water to drink.

B: Still or sparkling?

A: Still please.

B: Can we order? OK so that's one fish and chips and one hotpot. And could we also have a bottle of still mineral water? Oh and could you bring some ketchup? Thanks. (fade)

B: Did you enjoy your hotpot?

A: Yes I did, it was really delicious.

B: Now, would you like a dessert?

A: Oh no thanks I couldn't. The hotpot was very filling.

B: What about a coffee then?

A: Yes that would be nice, thanks. (fade)

B: Could we have the bill please? Now I would like to pay for this.

A: Oh no really, let me at least pay half.

B: No I insist. It's on me.

A: Well thank you very much. That's very kind of you.

B: Not at all.

Unit 6

A: What difficulties do business people tend to have when working in different cultures?

B: Well let me give you a few examples. From a cultural perspective people who come from other parts of the world and work in Britain need to know that we tend to say 'please' and 'thank you' a lot. If you don't use 'please' and 'thank you' people are considered impolite.

A: Yes, I suppose that's just the way we're brought up, we're taught …

B: Exactly. Conversely people in the Far East tend not to use eye contact, so a British person working there may find that impolite, but if we look them straight in the face they would think we were being impolite.

A: So it's really what you're conditioned to, what you think is right and wrong.

B: Exactly.

A: But what about cultural tips, are they absolutely vital? Is it important that you have a good understanding of other cultures?

B: It's a good question because what we tend to do is to provide generic cultural programmes. If you are working in a multicultural, multinational environment it's very difficult to learn all the aspects.

A: You can't know them all.

B: So we provide a generic framework. At the end of our courses we give them some very general tips that cover most cultures.

A: Can you give me some examples?

B: Things like being even more polite, even more formal than you would normally be in your own culture.

A: Right.

B: So you start off very formal when addressing somebody. People appreciate it if you're more formal. And things like, you should take time to learn people's names, their titles, the correct pronunciation, the least you can do is to learn how to say someone's name correctly.

A: What about tips on gift giving?

B: Yeah when you're out on a business trip, do you take a gift for your client or for their partner? Some cultures do; some don't. And if you do take a gift which one? Don't take alcohol to the Middle East obviously. Try not to give leather gifts if you're going to India, and flowers as well. You know in some cultures you can't give particular flowers.

A: But should you be aware of stereotyping people?

B: I think that's a good point. It's always good to bear in mind that that when we talk about cultural tips they are really only generalizations and there are always going to be exceptions. I think if anything the most important thing is keep that formality and respect … and smile, that's really important, and not showing anger. Nobody likes to see anger in any way.

A: And what about people's attitude to time? I know that that varies a lot from country to country. (fade)

1 He never quite got the deal because he worked in a very British / American way. He just flew in, had the meetings and flew out again. So we advised him to try spending a bit more time with his Italian colleagues, to establish more trust and understanding between them. We suggested he spent the night and went out for dinner with them which he did. And as a result the next time he went the deal was struck. In other cultures you go and meet people and they talk a lot. You think they're just talking for the sake of it. In fact what they're trying to do is get to know you, to see if they like you or want to work with you.

2 The essential thing about presentations is that they generally need to be short and succinct. A good structure makes it much easier to follow. So we basically taught him some basic presentation skills and gave him important phrases like 'the first thing I'd like to do is this, and finally …'. It certainly gave helped him to get his message across more clearly.

3 What we did was to teach the Dutch woman meeting strategies, for example how to interrupt in the right place, what to say when she interrupts and how to put a point across. These simple techniques gave her a lot more confidence and so she was able to assert herself more.

4 Well the problem here was really about communication. So we got the two women together and explained a few essentials. Firstly just because we do things one way in one country, it's not the only way of working. For example in Britain we use email a lot. We like written communication, whereas the French and Italians tend not to reply as quickly or will prefer to ring you as there is still more emphasis on the spoken word. We also suggested that a good communication strategy is to fit in with your counterpart's way of working. If their first approach to you is written, then you do the same.

(((6.3)))

a were / sir
b there / here

(((6.4)))

/ɜː/ were:	where, work, fork, world, learn, year, terms, director, first, thirty.
/ɔː/ brought:	taught, you're, courses, because, launch, colour, walk.
/ɪə/ here:	we're, wear, clearly, teach, really, deal, between.
/ɑː/ part:	our, tour, are, share, particular, market.

(((6.5)))

A: Sharif Priya.
B: Hi, Sharif this Marie Boulaigre from Protex. I'm having some difficulty configuring the Tetra VPN.
A: What seems to be the problem?
B: Well nearly every time I try to add a new client the system crashes.
A: To add a what, sorry?
A: A new client.
B: OK I'm with you. So you're saying it causes the system to crash?
A: That's right. It seems to crash quite regularly.
B: What exactly do you mean by 'regularly'?
A: Well for about two in three clients.
B: Right.
A: Then I'm also having problems downloading the thirteen point one network files.
B: Sorry, did you say thirteen point one, or thirty point one?
A: Thirteen point one.

B: Well, I think there must have been some problems during the installation. I think the best thing is if I come over and sort it out. Would Monday morning suit you?
A: Next Monday morning – OK.

(((6.6)))

C: Schneller Solutions. Good morning can I help you?
A: Yes, this is Marie Boulaigre from Protex. Could I speak to Sharif Priya please.
C: Sorry I didn't catch your name. Could you speak up a bit please. The line's bad.
A: Yes, it's Marie Boulaigre.
C: And where did you say you are ringing from?
A: Protex.
C: OK, thank you. Putting you through … I'm sorry, the line's busy at the moment. Do you want to leave a message?
A: Could you tell Sharif that Marie Boulaigre from Protex called, that's P-R-O-T-E-X, and that I need to rearrange our meeting for Tuesday rather than the Monday as originally planned.
C: That's Tuesday the fifth right?
A: Right. But if he needs to speak to me he can get me on 0207 395 6168. Extension 16.
C: Sixteen. That's one six?
A: That's it.
C: Can I read that back to you to make sure I've got everything?
A: Of course.
C: Marie Boulaigre – B-U-O …
A: No, B-O-U-, then L-A-I-G-R-E.
C: B-O-U-L-A-I-G-R-E. OK, from Protex. You want to rearrange the meeting for Tuesday the fifth, and Sharif can reach you on 0207 395 6168, extension 16.
A: That's it. Thanks very much. Bye.
C: Goodbye.

(((6.7)))

A: It would be much easier if you just went on our website where the instructions are.
B: Oh.
A: But anyway, basically, all you need to do is open the top cover of the printer, remove the toner cartridge, unpack the new one and install it in the same place.
B: Uh huh.
A: Right now hold the toner tight with both hands and rock it gently several times at a 45-degree angle. Then you need to bend the tab up and down several times down several times until it is detached from the cartridge.
B: Um, hang on a moment, I'm still opening the cartridge.
A: Well once you've done that you hold the tab firmly and pull it until the sealing tape comes out all the way. Then install the new toner by …

(((6.8)))

A: Well before you do anything you need to check that you've got the right type of toner cartridge for your machine.
B: Yes I have checked and it corresponds to the model number.
A: Good, and the other thing is to make sure that when you remove the cartridge you don't touch the transfer roller.
B: The what, sorry?
A: The transfer roller. If you open the cover of the printer, you'll see something metal and circular that looks like a tube. That's the transfer roller.

verbs

acknowledge /æk'nɒlɪdʒ/ *v* to report that you have received something

ban /bæn/ *v* to forbid something officially

block /blɒk/ *v* to prevent

crash /kræʃ/ *v* to drop in value suddenly as a result of loss in confidence in the market

sack /sæk/ *v* (informal) to dismiss someone from a job often because of poor performance or conduct

sign /saɪn/ *v* to write your name at the bottom of a legally binding agreement

slash /slæʃ/ *v* (informal) reduce

surge /sɜːdʒ/ *n* to rise suddenly

UNIT 10

nouns

annual leave /ænjuəl 'liːv/ *n* time absent from work taken during a year for non-health reasons

auction /'ɔːkʃn/ *n* method of selling things in which each item is sold to the person who offers the most money for it

back-up /'bæk ʌp/ *n* extra copy in case the original doesn't work

bid /bɪd/ *n* an offer to buy something, especially in competition with other buyers

bookmark /'bʊkmɑːk/ *n* a function that allows you to keep a special list of web page addresses on your browser so you can easily find them again

brochure /'brəʊʃə(r)/ *n* booklet or pamphlet containing information about something

browser /'braʊzə(r)/ *n* programme used for displaying web pages

call centre /'kɔːl sentə(r)/ *n* mass telephone service offered by organization or company in which people wanting information about a particular product or service can talk to someone directly

chatroom /'tʃætruːm/ *n* a place where you can talk to someone over the Internet, either one-to-one or many-to-many

cookie /'kʊki/ *n* a unique identifier or code sent to your browser when you access a particular site; the code enables the site to 'remember' the personal information you give and access it automatically each time you visit the site

corporate hospitality /kɔːprət hɒspɪ'tæləti/ *n* entertainment of company clients

corporate values /kɔːprət 'væljuːz/ *n* standards and ethics of a company

encryption /ɪn'krɪpʃn/ *n* changing date into a secret code – when the data is encrypted it is translated into a code which is impossible to understand without a key

fall /fɔːl/ *n* (American English) autumn

firewall /'faɪəwɔːl/ *n* a security system used by many companies to prevent outsiders from accessing internal networks

fraud /frɔːd/ *n* act of not telling the truth in order to illegally obtain something

guideline /'ɡaɪdlaɪn/ *n* advice on the way to do something generally given by an expert

hacker /'hækə(r)/ *n* a person who uses computers for a hobby, especially to break into other people's computer systems

helpline /'helplaɪn/ *n* telephone service for customers who need help with a particular product or service provided

homepage /'həʊmpeɪdʒ/ *n* the main webpage for a business, organization, or person

jargon /'dʒɑːɡən/ *n* technical or specialized words used in a particular profession

mailing list /'meɪlɪŋ lɪst/ *n* a list of all the email addresses to which information is sent on a regular basis

maintenance /'meɪntənəns/ *n* the process of keeping something in good working order

merger /'mɜːdʒə(r)/ *n* unification of two companies

niche market /niːʃ 'mɑːkɪt/ *n* a market for very specialized goods or services

password /'pɑːswɜːd/ *n* a secret word to enable you to gain access to an account on a computer

portal /'pɔːtəl/ *n* an all-in-one super website containing a collection of related information services

promotion /prə'məʊʃn/ *n* being raised to a higher position within a company, e.g. from junior manager to senior manager

spam /spæm/ *n* material, such as advertisements and jokes, which you receive by email, and which you haven't asked for and don't want, the online equivalent of junk mail

surfer /'sɜːfə(r)/ *n* (informal) someone who visits many webpages

tour company /'tɔː kʌmpəni/ *n* operator that organizes travel

virus /'vaɪrəs/ *n* a code which is hidden inside a program or email message; when the program is opened, the virus spreads quickly and destroys or corrupts the system and / or the data it contains.

verbs

bid /bɪd/ *v* to offer to buy something, especially in competition with other buyers

claim /kleɪm/ *v* to demand or ask for something

claim compensation /kleɪm kɒmpen'seɪʃn/ *v* to claim money to pay for the effect the effects of damage

claim expenses /kleɪm ɪk'spensɪz/ *v* ask for money back from your company after you have spent money for working purposes

click through /klɪk 'θruː/ *v* to go from one link to another on a website

merge /mɜːdʒ/ *v* to join two companies together

run out /rʌn 'aʊt/ *v* to use up or finish a supply of something

take over /teɪk 'əʊvə(r)/ *v* to gain control of a company by buying it or controlling enough of its shares

undercharge /ʌndə'tʃɑːdʒ/ *v* not to charge the full amount

adjectives

high-tech /haɪ 'tek/ *adj* involving 'high' (advanced) technology

off sick /ɒf 'sɪk/ *adj* not at work due to being ill / sick

Acknowledgements

The author and publisher are grateful to those who have given permission to reproduce the following extracts and adaptations of copyright material:

pp 6–7 Extracts from *Funky Business* by Jonas Ridderstråle and Kjell Nordstrøm Reproduced by permission of Pearson Education Limited.

p 10 Interview with Juliet Soskice. Reproduced by permission of Juliet Soskice.

p 20 Interview with Tim Watson. Reproduced by permission of Tim Watson.

p 27 'It's becoming a mad ad World' by Caroline E. Mayer © 2000 The Washington Post. Reproduced by permission of The Washington Post Writers Group.

p 31 Interview with Martin Addison. Reproduced by permission of Martin Addison.

pp 36–37 Extracts from *Global Forces: A Guide for Enlightened Leaders* by Bruce Nixon. Reproduced by permission of Management Books 2000 Limited.

p 39 Information about Fairtrade Foundation. Reproduced by permission.

p 42 Extracts from *Essential Managers: Managing Meetings* (Dorling Kindersley 1998), copyright © 1998 Dorling Kindersley Limited, text copyright © 1998 Tim Hindle. Reproduced by permission of The Penguin Group (UK).

pp 46–47 Interview with Hamish McRae. Reproduced by permission of Hamish McRae.

p 48 Extracts from *America's Stupidest Business Decisions* by Bill Adler, Jr. and Julie Houghton © Bill Adler, Jr. and Julie Houghton. Reproduced by permission of HarperCollins Publishers Inc.

p 48 Extracts from *The Book of Heroic Failures: The Official Handbook of the Not Terribly Good Club of Great Britain* by Stephen Pile (Routledge 1979, Viking, 1989) Copyright © Stephen Pile. Reproduced by permission of the Estate of Angela Carter c/o Rogers, Coleridge and White Ltd and The Penguin Group (UK).

p 56 Interview with Sue Hyde. Reproduced by permission of Sue Hyde.

p 68 Extracts from *The Financial Times Guide to Business Travel* by Stuart Crainer and Des Dearlove (eds.) © Pearson Education Limited 2001. Reproduced by permission.

p 70 Interview with Samantha Day. Reproduced by permission of Samantha Day.

p 76 Interview with Kathryn Dighton. Reproduced by permission of Kathryn Dighton.

p 81 'Permission Marketing: Review' by Eugene Eric Kim, *New Architect*, April 2000. Reproduced by permission of *New Architect*.

p 86 Interview with David Smith. Reproduced by permission of David Smith.

p 92 'Negotiating' questionnaire by Brenda Townsend Hall created with Hot Potatoes © Half-Baked Software. Reproduced by permission.

p 96 Extracts from *Architects of the Business Revolution: The Ultimate E-Business Book* by Des Dearlove and Stephen Coomber. © John Wiley and Sons Limited. Reproduced by permission.

p 97 'Are we all speaking the same language' by David Wilford, The Times 20 April 2000. Reproduced by permission of Times Newspapers Limited.

p 98 Interview with Alex Czajikowski. Reproduced by permission of Alex Czajikowski.

Although every effort has been made to trace and contact copyright holders before publication, this has not been possible in some cases. We apologize for any apparent infringement of copyright and if notified, the publisher will be pleased to rectify any errors or omissions at the earliest opportunity.

Sources:

p 26 *Evening Standard* 7 December 1998

p 28 *The Wiley Book of Business Quotations*

pp 11, 32, and 99 *A Guide to Listening* by Ian MacKay

p 38 *Guardian Weekly* 8-14 February 2001

p 40 *Sunday Express* 4 March 2001

p 41 *Daily Mail* 25 February 2000

p 47 *The Year 2000* by Herman Kahn and Anthony J. Wiener.

p 52 *Business Life* December 1997 / January 1998

p 58 SIETAR, Houston

p 58 (How to be Late) *Communication Between Cultures* by Larry Samovar & Richard Porter

p 58 (Working 9–5?) EIRO

p 59 (Working 8 Days a Week) *The Observer* 7 April 1996

p 59 (All Work and No Play) *Sociology: Themes and Perspectives* by Michael Haralambos, Martin Holborn and Robin Herald

pp 27 and 69 *In One Day*, Capstone Publishing

p 71 *Sunday Telegraph* 11 March 2001

p 73 *Business Life* July / August 2000

p 89 *The Economist* 22 August 2001

p 92 *The Ultimate Lists Book* by Geoff Tibballs

p 100 *Guardian* 31 October 1998

p 102 *One Stop Customer Care*, Prentice Hall Europe / ICSA Publishing.

The publisher would like to thank the following for the use of photographs:

Ace Photo Agency p 90 (Bill Bachman/car sale); Alamy pp 58 (Garry Gay), 93 (IMAGINA/Atsushi Tsunoda), 103 (Robert Llewellyn/organiser, Michael Foyle/river); ©Babel Language and Cultural Consultants p 56 (logo); Bridgeman Art Library pp 26 (092253 Posters at Trouville, 1906 (oil on canvas) (detail) by Raoul Dufy (1877-1953). Musee National d'Art Moderne, Paris, France/Bridgeman Art Library. ©ADAGP, Paris and DACS, London 2002. CNAC/MNAM Dist. RMN), 36 (58898 The Mint, from Aristotle's 'Ethics, Politics, Economics, from a French Translation by Nicholas Oreme (vellum) (detail). Bibliotheque Municipale, Rouen, France/ Bridgeman Art Library), 56 (All77432 Sistine Chapel Ceiling: Creation of Adam, detail of the outstretched arms, 1510 (fresco) (post-restoration) by Michelangelo Buonarroti (1475-1564). Vatican Museums and Galleries, Vatican City, Italy/Bridgeman Art Library), 76 (NUL112297 Campbell's Soup Cans, 1965 (silkscreen on canvas) by Andy Warhol (1930-87). Private Collection/Bridgeman Art Library. ©The Andy Warhol Foundation for the Visual Arts, Inc./DACS, London, 2002. Trademarks Licensed by Campbell Soup Company. All Rights Reserved), 96 (ASC140134 Vegetable Seller (Sabzi-farosh) c.1890 (w/c on paper) (detail) by Wassilij Ivanowitsch Nawasoff (20th century) Royal Asiatic Society, London, UK/Bridgeman Art Library); CORBIS pp 67 (©Michael Prince/male), 104 (©Anton Daix/female); ©Dorling Kindersley p 42 (Essential Managers: Managing Meetings by Tim Hindle); ©EasyJet p 70; Mary Evans Picture Library p 41; ©Fair Trade pp 38, 39; ©Ferrari p 20 (cars); Format p 30 (©Maggie Murray); gettyimages/FPG International p 64 (Justin Pumfrey); gettyimages/ImageBank pp 8 (Britt Erlanson/female), 13 (Yang China Tourism Press. Liu/female), 44 (Romilly Lockyer), 45 (Romilly Lockyer), 52 (Rita Maas/caviar), 65 (Peter Hendrie/Sydney), 66 (Eric Meola), 68 (Peter Cade), 69 (Yellow Dog Productions), 72 (Guido Alberto Rossi/Hassan II Mosque, Andrea Pistolesi/market), 103 (Antonio M.Rosario); gettyimages/Image Bank/Infocus International. Morrell. Infocus p24; gettyimages/PhotoDisc pp 10 (Ryan McVay), 13 (Stephanie Hafner/office), 23 (Keith Brofsky), 32 (Keith Brofsky), 88 (Janis Christie), 92 (Jeff Maloney), 98 (Don Farrall); gettyimages/Stone pp 8 (Julie Toy/male), 13 (Jon Riley/male), 49 (Adrain Weinbrecht), 52 (Angela Wyant/garlic), 62 (Jeff Zaruba), 65 (Peter Mason/male), 72 (Nicholas DeVore/Valle'du Dades), 86 (Steven Weiberg/abacus), 90 (Christopher Bissell/fruit stall, Bruce Ayres/males), 104 (David Hanover/male); ©Seth Godin p 80; Ronald Grant Archive p 83; ImageState pp 67 (AGE Fotostock/female), 84; ©Hamish McRae pp 46, 47 (The World in 2020 by Hamish McRae, published by Harper Collins, ISBN: 0-00-255197-7; ©MUJI p 77; The Photographers Library pp 6 (photolibrary.com), 16 (Candice Farmer); Rex Features p 17 (Rex Rystedt); Science Photo Library p 46 (Luke Dodd); ©David Smith p 86; ©Juliet Soskice p 10; Video Arts p 31; View pp 84 (©Peter Cook/Victorian offices, ©Grant Smith/modern offices); ©Tim Watson p 20.

The following picture was taken on commission for OUP:

Trever Clifford p39 (Fairtrade/coffee bags)

The publisher would like to thank the following for their permission allowing use to reproduce the copyright cartoon:
©The 5th Wave, www.the5thwave.com p 32.

Illustrations by:

Francis Blake/Three In A Box pp 9, 15, 22, 33, 42, 63; Kate Charlesworth pp 99, 100; Mark Duffin pp 48, 79; Michael Fischer pp 85, 101, 111, 115; Ian Mitchell p 28; Simeon Stout p 51; Stephanie Wunderlich pp 53, 73.

The author and publisher are grateful to the following individuals who read and piloted the material:

Rachel Appleby, Martin Bradbeer, Aneta Dybska, Sandra Goodall, Michael Jeive, Jon Kear

Author's acknowledgements

My biggest thanks go to Anna Southern for organizing and conducting all the interviews, and for her huge input towards the writing of the book. I would also like to thank Rebecca Chapman, Janet Schantz and Jacquie Dutcher for their input on the email course; Jacqueline Landi, Aleksandra Pazurek, and Petra Neumeier for insights into their languages; and Martin Gandy, Angus Brogdon, Richard Wallwork and Jackie Rymell for providing business materials, and the interviewees for their time and information.

A final thanks to Helen Forrest and Anna Cowper for their editorial work and unending patience.